# I WANT TO BE RICH!
# FINANCIAL PLANNING FOR TEENS

Karin Humbolt

The Reynolds Publishing Company

Overland Park, Kansas

I WANT TO BE RICH!  FINANCIAL PLANNING FOR TEENS

2nd Edition

Written by Karin Humbolt

Library of Congress Preassigned Control Number 2017938031

ISBN-13: 978-0-9665128-4-7

Published and distributed in the United States of America by:

The Reynolds Publishing Company
P.O. Box 13535
Overland Park, Kansas 66282

Printed in the United States of America

# This book is dedicated

as always to my father, a kind and loving man who showed me the way.

*I Want To Be Rich! Financial Planning for Teens* was originally inspired by a money management seminar taught to a teacher-client's 10th grade class. The day of the seminar I was besieged with questions from teenagers like you. That day I learned a valuable lesson. Teenagers have as much curiosity, questions, and misconceptions about money and investments as adults.

In 1998 my first financial planning book for teens entitled, *I Want To Be Rich! A Teenager's Modem To Money* was published. The response to this book was heartwarming!

And in 2007 a Spanish translation entitled *¡Quiero Ser Rico!...Planificación Financiera Para Jóvenes* was published.

For excerpts from the *New York Times Sunday* edition, *Miami Herald - Money Q & A*, and *Criticas*, please see the back cover of this book.

*I Want To Be Rich! Financial Planning for Teens* is not a story of how to be a billionaire or the richest person on the planet. It is a philosophy of how to live your life. To achieve a solid financial future, be persistent. Never give up! Be kind to others.

**K.H.**

## ACKNOWLEDGEMENTS

Thank you to Angie Alaya for the cover design of this book. Many thanks to Steve Gilbreath for his illustrated drawings of "Hal." To Jackie Kraft, M. S. Ed., editor of the first edition, for her kind help and encouragement. And to all my friends who have shared their dreams and allowed me to be a part of those dreams.

# TABLE OF CONTENTS

# CHAPTER 1

# INTRODUCTION

## Balance Your Life & Your Money

Have you ever wanted to buy something badly and not been able to afford it?  If the answer is "Yes," then *I Want To Be Rich! ... Financial Planning For Teens* is the book for you.

Do you like money?  Do you hear teachers, journalists, or friends speak about the stock market and wonder what they're talking about?  Does the name **Dow Jones Industrial Average** make as much sense as that foreign language class you can't quite grasp?  If your answer is "Yes," this is the book for you.

Do you want to go to college, but don't know how you or your parents can afford it? Are you interested in getting a job, yet don't know how to get one that pays more than minimum wage? Do you have enough money?

These are a few of the subjects that are covered in this book about the spending, saving, and investment of money ... otherwise known as money management.

As a **net worth advisor**, I helped adults achieve financial freedom. Many of my clients were educators, including university professors and high school teachers. My clients were no different than you when it comes to their knowledge or lack of knowledge about investments and the management of money.

Years ago, when I was very young, I inherited some money. The result? I spent it very quickly on **frivolous** things. If I had invested the money, that $20,000 would today be worth approximately $41,500 if it averaged a 5% **return**; $83,500 if it averaged a 10% return; and $163,000 if it averaged a 15% return!

At the time, it seemed like a good idea. Trust me, money spends easier than it is acquired. I became a net worth advisor so I'd never make that mistake again!

My interest in writing this book was spurred by a request from a teacher/client to conduct a money management seminar for her tenth-grade class. After my presentation, I was besieged with questions from teens like yourself. The questions asked ranged from how to balance a checkbook to what is a mutual fund.

I learned a valuable lesson that day. Teenagers have as much curiosity, questions, and misconceptions about money and investments as adults!

If I could show you how to make $1,000,000, would you be interested? Most people would be interested. However, with the price of goods and services rising (a common occurrence known as *inflation*) a million dollars might not be enough. Difficult to believe? That's the point of this book ... to help you understand money management and the making of money from money in simple language.

Please keep in mind, this book is a basic money management primer for teens. This is only a beginning to what you should spend a lifetime exploring ... money, how to keep it, save it, and make money from it.

My intention is to give you suggestions to take the mystery out of money management. How to start good saving and spending habits, some do's and don'ts about investments, and tips for accumulating more money in the long run than your parents or grandparents.

The circular sign that the cartoon character "Hal" is holding at the beginning of this chapter is the symbol for **yin and yang**, a Chinese theory that says for every action there is an opposite reaction. Yin and yang represent the need for balance. When it comes to money management, we also need balance.

You should be pleased to know that the best secret to accumulating money and wealth is time! And as a teen, time is on your side. While the secret of time alone will not make you a millionaire, if you practice this book's tips and suggestions, you will know more about money and the making of money than most adults.

Throughout this book, you will see words *italicized* and highlighted in **bold type**. The definition of these words is in the Glossary at the back of this book. If a word is not in the Glossary and you don't understand the term, check the definition in your dictionary. This practice of studying the definitions of unfamiliar words will help you to better understand the subject matter.

I recommend that you keep notebook paper, pens, and pencils nearby while reading this book. Some chapters include practice exercises that will require writing materials.

The *Information Resources* included at the back of this book will further increase your knowledge of money management. I suggest you make use of these sources of information.

How do we get started toward the accumulation of money? Read on to *Chapter 2 – Setting Goals*!

# CHAPTER 2

# SETTING GOALS

## Your First Step To Financial Freedom

The accumulation of money first and foremost involves the act of setting and **implementing** goals.

*Webster's New World Dictionary* defines the word goal as: "1. the line or place at which a race, trip, etc. is ended; 2. an object or end that one strives to attain; aim."

Why set goals? Because you need a beginning and a destination! If you don't know what you are aiming for or where you are going, the chance of achieving anything substantial is slim to none.

Imagine you are taking a vacation to a place where you've never traveled before. If you don't know your destination or don't have a road map, your journey could be difficult.

Setting goals is the perfect way to start your journey toward financial success. Your goals will be your road map to financial freedom!

**Here are some questions to ask yourself before setting goals:**

1. **What financial goals do I want to achieve?** Do I want to buy a cell phone, new clothes, a computer, a car, pay for college, live on my own, buy a house, save for retirement?

2. **When do I want to achieve my financial goals?** Next week, next month, in a year, five years? The more time you have, the easier it is to achieve your goals.

3. **How will I achieve my goals?** The answer to this question will be the nuts and bolts that make your goals and dreams come true.

I suggest setting both short-term and long-term goals. For many adults, short-term goals may include time periods of one to five years. As a teenager, your time frame for short-term goals may be considerably shorter ... say one to six months and up to one year.

Long-term goals for adults are five years and longer, say ten, twenty, or even thirty years. That's probably unrealistic for you at this stage. For purposes of discussion, let's consider your long-term goals to be one to five years. Now let's get started.

**The most important rule for setting goals is:**

- **Write your goals on paper! Repeat after me. Write your goals on paper!**

Let's start with a short-term goal exercise. Sit at a table with this book, pens and your notebook. **Ask yourself the following questions:**

- **What do I want to buy?**

- **How much will it cost?**

- **When do I want, or need it?** Be realistic.

- **How will I earn the money?**

As you answer each question, number and write down your answers. **For example:**

1. **What do I want to buy?** A digital camera.

2. **How much will it cost?** $400.

3. **When do I want it?** In three months for vacation.

You want to purchase a new digital camera that costs $400 in three months. Three months equals twelve weeks. Divide $400 by twelve weeks. $400 / 12 weeks = $33.33 per week. **Therefore, you will need to save $33.33 each week to purchase the item.**

4. **How will I earn the money?** Allowance. Chores for parents, adult relatives, neighbors, or adult friends of parents. A part-time job.

**Now let's cover long-term goals:**

1. **What do I want to buy?** A car.

2. **How much will it cost?** $5,000.

3. **When do I want, or need it?** (Next week, but Mom and Dad won't let you drive until you're sixteen.) Three years.

You want to purchase a car that costs $5,000 in three years. We're talking used car. What is realistic is obtainable. $5,000 divided by 3 years equals $1,667 per year. $1,667 divided by 52 weeks per year equals $32.06 per week.

$$\$5,000 \;/\; 3 \text{ years} = \$1,667 \text{ per year}$$

$$\$1,667 \;/\; 52 \text{ weeks} = \$32.06 \text{ per week}$$

Does $32.06 per week seem more obtainable than $5,000? Of course, if Mom and Dad read this over your shoulder, they will probably add other costs you may not have considered ... like taxes, licenses and insurance. Not to worry, we'll cover that in *Chapter 4 - Making A Budget ... It's Not A Puzzle.*

**4.  How will I earn the money?** The answer to this question is similar to the answer for short-terms goals. Allowance. Chores for parents, adult relatives, neighbors, or adult friends of parents. Part-time job or full-time summer job.

When deciding "How will I earn the money?" for short or long-term goals, be creative. For instance, many parts of the United States experience snow days. Next time you're missing a day at school due to snow, why not play the part of **entrepreneur**? Instead of social media or watching television, make money shoveling snow from driveways and sidewalks. You may be surprised by the number of jobs you acquire from adults who are either elderly, lazy, out of shape, or too busy to shovel the snow themselves.

In addition, many adults are starting small businesses from home. A small business requires the typing and filing of documents. And clerical work is an easier job than shoveling snow!

Note: Interested in being an entrepreneur and owning your own business? We'll cover this subject in *Chapter 15 – You're The Boss.*

For each of your goals, complete the above exercise. Make two separate lists. One for short-term goals and the second for long-term goals. Don't set too many goals at once. Start with one or two goals in each category.

**The second rule of setting goals is:**

- **Review your goals often. In other words, don't write your goals in the notebook and misplace it.**

Reviewing your goals once a day is a good habit to establish. Take five minutes and read your goals and how you will achieve those goals out loud. Yes ... say your goals aloud. Look into a mirror as you recite your goals. This is a good reinforcement of your goals.

In Napoleon Hill's book, *Think And Grow Rich*, the importance of repeating goals to yourself daily is discussed. Through repetition your goals will register not only in your conscious mind, but also in your subconscious mind. In other words, when you live, breathe, and feel your goals, you will also begin to achieve your goals.

**The third rule of setting goals is:**

- **Revise your goals only as needed.**

Choose your goals with plenty of thought and stick to them. However, changing situations may necessitate the changing of your goals from time to time. I don't recommend changing your goals often or without plenty of thought. If you do need to revise some of your financial goals, return to the goal setting exercise and repeat the steps.

**In review, to determine and achieve your goals:**

- **Write your goals on paper.**

- **Review your goals often.**

- **Revise your goals only as needed.**

One of the first financial goals you should set for yourself is a regular savings plan. Read on to *Chapter 3 - Saving and Investing,* and you will be on your way to financial independence.

# CHAPTER 3

# SAVING AND INVESTING

## Time Is On Your Side

Now that we've discussed the importance of setting goals, it's important to make saving and investing one of *your* goals. Systematic saving and investment is the practice of saving and/or investing money on a regular basis. This can be weekly or monthly.

If you learn one thing from this book, plan to establish and stick with a regular saving and investment plan.

Why save on a regular basis you ask? The reason is this. If you don't save first, before spending your money, you may never start saving ... or at least not until it's too late.

As a teenager, time is on your side. That statement is correct because a secret to accumulating wealth and money is to start early!

For instance, suppose you invested $2,000 at 17 years of age in a traditional **Individual Retirement Account (IRA)** and never invested again. You also did not touch that investment until you retire at 55 years of age, or 38 years later.

Depending upon the source, the historical rate of return for the major stock indexes from the 1920's to today have averaged from 10% to 12% a year.

Let's be conservative and assume your investment had a 10% average annual rate of return. After 38 years your $2,000 investment at an annual return of 10% could grow to $74,808. If the annual return was 12%, your $2,000 investment could grow to $148,359. **That's what I mean by "time is on your side!"**

To start your saving and investment plan, select a fixed percentage of your allowance or salary as your savings goal. Before you spend a dime of that allowance or salary, put your savings into a bank savings account. Saving first translates into, "pay yourself first!"

**The theory of "pay yourself first" works on the principle of, "if you don't pay yourself first, nobody's going to do it for you."** This is true for teenagers as well as adults.

When deciding an amount to save on a regular basis, be realistic. Realistic … there's that word again. However, there's not much sense in attempting to save 20% of your allowance each month if you're always withdrawing from the savings account because you're running short of spending cash.

Americans are notoriously skimpy savers. A 2015 Market Watch.com article stated that, "62% of Americans have less than $1,000 in their savings accounts and 21% don't even have a saving account."

When deciding what amount of your income you will save, be realistic. Save as much as possible, but most importantly, start saving something on a regular basis.

**Why save or invest?** Making money from money is the only way most people can earn money without physically working for it.

There are numerous ways to make money from money. At this stage, you're probably most familiar with saving money in a savings account at a local bank. Most banks in the United States are federally insured, which means you are guaranteed by the full faith and credit of the United States government to receive back whatever you put into your savings account plus interest.

The drawback to saving in a bank savings account is the interest paid by the bank is low compared to other types of investment earnings. Interest on bank savings accounts can range from 1.5% to 3%. Interest this low won't make anyone wealthy.

However, keeping a bank savings account for short-term savings goals and emergencies is a good idea. In fact, it's convenient because your money is easily accessible, it's guaranteed, and usually you won't pay a penalty for withdrawing your money.

Another method of saving is investing in U.S. savings bonds. When the bond is cashed at **maturity**, you will be paid the face amount of the bond. The face amount equals the amount paid for the bond plus interest.

Some people like to save by investing in real estate. A drawback to real estate investment is the large amount of **down payment** that's often needed to get started. If you borrow money from a bank to buy a house, most lending institutions will require as much as 20% for a down payment, which can be a hefty amount. We'll discuss more about real estate in *Chapter 11 – Real Estate ... The American Dream*.

Some people turn to stamp or coin collections, baseball cards, antiques, or gold and silver **bullion** as investments. These types of investments can be risky and are only recommended for investors willing to thoroughly research the investment.

As you may be aware, millions of Americans and people all over the world invest in the stock market. A person who invests in the stock market basically owns a piece of the company whose **stock** he purchases. We'll discuss the stock market in *Chapter 8 – Stocks ... The Place To Be*.

Other people choose to own a piece of hundreds of different companies by investing in **mutual funds**. We'll discuss mutual funds in *Chapter 9 – Mutual Funds ... Convenient Investing*.

If an individual prefers an investment that pays a steady income, she may choose to invest in government or corporate **bonds**. The subject of bonds will be covered in *Chapter 7 – Bonds ... The*

*Conservative Investment.*

Whatever method of investment you choose, it's important to learn as much as possible about that type of investment. Become an expert when it comes to your investments.

At this stage, it is best to open your own savings account at a bank, savings and loan association, or credit union. Shop around by visiting several different banks. Ask what rate of interest each bank pays and any other features available to you by opening a savings account. Comparison shopping is good because the amount of interest paid may vary at each savings institution.

**Having your own savings account, as well as a checking account, builds good *credit*.** Having good credit will help you obtain loans for cars, college, an apartment, or a home in the future. We'll discuss this subject in more detail in *Chapter 16 - Credit & Credit Cards ... A Word of Caution.*

As mentioned previously, choose a percentage of your allowance or income from your job as your savings goal. Or you may want to choose a certain dollar amount. **It is not important how much you save, just get into the habit of saving!**

Your savings goal can be for short-term financial goals, long-term financial goals, and for emergency money. Whatever the purpose, saving is a very important habit that should stay with you all your life. The sooner you start your savings habit, the better!

**Remember to:**

- **Pay yourself first!**

- **Decide on a definite savings amount.**

- **Stick with your savings program.**

For tips on how much you should save and spend, read on to *Chapter 4 - Making A Budget ... It's Not A Puzzle!*

# CHAPTER 4

# MAKING A BUDGET

## It's Not A Puzzle

Have you ever taken a trip to a place you've never been before? Would you search and struggle, to find your way like someone in the dark without a light? It would make more sense to follow a road map to reach your destination. This is the case with a financial plan. To reach your financial goals, it's important to have a financial roadmap ... otherwise known as a budget.

In this chapter, we will develop three monthly budgets. First, we will design a budget to fit your present circumstances, known as "**Your Budget Now.**" Second, we will make adjustments to help you learn how to live within a budget, known as "**Your Adjusted Budget.**" Third, we will design a futuristic budget for when you go to college or live on your own. This budget is known as "**On Your Own Budget.**"

Let's get started with your personalized budget! **Complete the following exercise to track your spending habits.**

**1. Each day in your notebook record every purchase and the amount spent.**

**2. Continue this exercise for one month.**

**3. At the end of the month, total your expenses.** By tracking your expenses, you will get an accurate record of how much you are spending each month.

Keeping track of all your expenses in writing is an eye-opening experience. This exercise will reveal why you are often short of money, even if you have a job. When you discover what you are buying and how much it costs, you are ready to design a budget for your present circumstances ... "Your Budget Now."

On a sheet of paper, make a column on the left-hand side labeled "Income". Underneath and several lines down label the next column "Expenses."

Under the "Income" column write the source and amount of money you earn monthly. Monthly income includes your allowance, money from part-time and full-time jobs, gifts from relatives, etc. When designing any budget, money from jobs will be **net income**. That is your income after all taxes have been taken out.

Under the "Expenses" column list your expenses and the monthly dollar amounts. Expenses include:

1. **Savings.** Determine the amount of money, percentage of income, or dollar amount you will save each month. Label this item "Savings" and enter the dollar amount. It does not matter if the amount is only $1.00 per month! Get into the habit of saving on a regular basis. In this manner, you will learn to save for those upcoming concert tickets, clothes, a car, college funds, or whatever you need to save for in the future.

2. **Tithing.** This is the practice of contributing a percentage of your income to the religious organization of your choice.

3. **Personal items.** Shampoo, make-up, haircuts, and clothing.

**4.   Entertainment costs.**  Movies, concerts and sporting event tickets.

**5.   Food.**  Meals away from home, snacks, lunches, and dinners out.

**6.   Transportation costs.**  Mass transit, cab fares, car expenses such as gasoline, oil changes, maintenance, repairs, car payments, insurance, auto tags and licenses.

**7.   Miscellaneous expenses.**  Any other expenses.

Now total all expenses at the bottom of the budget worksheet. If you have some quarterly, semi-annual, or annual expenses, divide the amount by the appropriate number of months to arrive at a monthly dollar amount.  For example:  If car insurance costs $600 semi-annually, divide the $600 by 6 months to arrive at a cost of $100 per month for automobile insurance.

On the following "Your Budget Now" example, the teen has something in common with many Americans today.  This individual spends more money than he is earning, as you can see by the ***net loss*** of $159.00 per month.

# YOUR BUDGET NOW

## INCOME

| | | |
|---|---|---|
| Allowance | $  40.00 | |
| Part-time job (net) | $200.00 | |
| **Total Income** | | **$240.00** |

## EXPENSES

| | | |
|---|---|---|
| Savings (10%) | $  24.00 | |
| Personal | $  60.00 | |
| Entertainment | $  80.00 | |
| Food | $  75.00 | |
| Transportation | $160.00 | |
| **Total Expenses** | | **($399.00)** |
| **Net Gain** | | **$0** |
| **Net Loss  [$240 + ($399)] =** | | **($159.00) per month** |

At the bottom of your budget, subtract your total expenses from your total income. Are you trying to live beyond your income? If your expenses are more than your income, you will need to make adjustments. Here are some suggestions:

- **Sacrifice some of your entertainment by going out less or by finding less expensive alternatives.** This may be a painful option, but for some teenagers it is the only category where expenses can be lowered.

- **Work more hours, or find a better paying job.**

- **Negotiate a larger allowance by taking on additional job responsibilities at home.**

- **Eat out less.** Cooking at home is healthier and less expensive than eating out.

- **If you drive a car, watch your gasoline consumption.** Cruising eats $$$.

The following "Adjusted Budget" provides tips for an income that exceeds expenses. For instance, our teenager *negotiates* with parents to receive a larger allowance in exchange for tackling more jobs at home. The larger allowance accounts for $40.00 additional income per month.

Entertainment expenses were originally high compared to the amount of income. By renting movies instead of going to theatres and by watching sport events on mobile devices instead of in person, our teenager saves $40 a month.

Food expense was also high. By eating more at home, our teenager cut this expense by $45.00 per month.

Cost cutting also took place with transportation. With less cruising, transportation costs were cut by $60.00 per month. Or the teen could use mass transit.

Since savings is based on 10% of income, the monthly savings has now increased to $28.00 per month. Due to the increase of income and decrease in expenses, our teenager now has a **net gain** of $22.00 instead of a net loss!

# ADJUSTED BUDGET

## INCOME

Allowance              $  80.00

Part-time job (net)  $200.00

**Total Income**                              **$280.00**

## EXPENSES

Savings (10%)        $  28.00

Personal                $  60.00

Entertainment       $  40.00

Food                      $  30.00

Transportation      $100.00

**Total Expenses**                          **$258.00**

**Net Gain   [$280 - $258] =**         **$  22.00 per month**

**Net Loss**                                    **$    0**

No doubt you can think of some income increasing and expense cutting ideas. Under no circumstances do I suggest sacrificing homework or fun time. Instead work your budget smarter!

Once you've created a budget for your present circumstance, start work on a futurist budget. The purpose of "On Your Own Budget" is to learn how a budget works if you live on your own or attend higher education. This budget exercise should give you a new perspective on what goods and services actually cost. Far too often where money is concerned, it's "easy come, easy go."

We'll begin this budget much the same way we did "Your Budget Now." On a new sheet of notebook paper, list "Expenses" on the left and the monthly dollar amount to the right (see "Living On Your Own Budge" on a following page).

You may not be familiar with the costs of living on your own. Therefore, research the cost of these expenses. Most of this research can be done online or by calling and asking questions. For purposes of explanation, I'll supply some dollar amounts. However, to benefit the most from this exercise, do your own research.

**The following are suggestions for developing "On Your**

**Own Budget":**

1. **Allocate a set percentage of your income for savings.** Since *hypothetically* you are living on your own for the first time, you'll probably need most of your money to survive. Therefore, let's use 3% of income for savings with that equaling $60.00 per month.

2. **If you're living on your own, you'll need a place to live.** How much would rent cost for an apartment? If you don't know, contact several apartment complexes and ask what the monthly rent for a small apartment would cost.

3. **While you're speaking with the apartment manager, ask what utilities are included in the rent.** Utilities could include electricity, natural gas, water, sewer, trash, and cable. If you, as the tenant, must pay some or all utilities, ask the manager what the cost of utilities averages per month. Or call the local utility company and ask what utilities average per month for an apartment in that area.

4. **The cost of food.** Write down everything you eat in a week, at home or out. Check the cost of the food at the grocery store, total it for the week, and multiply by four weeks to get the monthly cost of food at home. You should include the basics like

vegetables, fruits, bread, milk, nuts, and meat. Next add the cost of food you eat out such as fast foods and home delivered pizza.

**5. Transportation costs.** This category will be moderate to very expensive depending upon the mode of transportation you choose. If you choose public transportation this expense may be relatively inexpensive.

a. Do you want a *new* car? The car payment for a $30,000 car could be over $500 per month. For our example, we used a $350 per month car payment for a used car.

b. Next, you'll need car insurance so you can legally drive this vehicle. The more expensive the car, the more expensive the insurance! You've probably heard insurance for teenagers is expensive. It is! For our example, we'll use $100 per month. Ask insurance agents what auto insurance for a teenager your age would cost for the car you want to purchase.

c. If you're going to the trouble of buying this car and paying for the insurance, you're going to need gasoline. A car also requires upkeep that includes regular oil changes and maintenance.

6.   **Clothing.**  If you live in a moderate climate, this expense could be less than for people living in northern states that require both winter and summer clothing.  Look at the price tags where you shop.  Estimate what was paid in a year for your clothes and divide by 12 months.

7.   **Personal items.**  Shampoo, soap, toothpaste, deodorant, make-up, razors, mouthwash, etc.  Price these items at grocery, drug, retail and discount stores.

8.   **Entertainment.**  Concert tickets, sporting events, movie tickets and rentals, golf fees, trips and vacations.

Once you learn what your expenses will include and how much they will cost, add them together.  This will give you a realistic picture what it costs to live on your own and how much income you will need to earn.

# LIVING ON YOUR OWN BUDGET

## Monthly Expenses

| | |
|---|---|
| Savings and Investments (3%) | $ 60.00 |
| Rent | $ 750.00 |
| Utilities (electricity, natural gas & cable) | $ 95.00 |
| Food | $ 160.00 |
| Transportation (car payment, insurance, gasoline & maintenance) | $ 535.00 |
| Clothing | $ 65.00 |
| Personal | $ 40.00 |
| Entertainment | $ 45.00 |
| **Total Expenses** | **$1,750.00** |

Remember these expenses are basic. We'll assume:

- You have furniture to furnish the apartment, dishes, tableware, pots, pans and skillets.

- You've already paid the apartment security deposit.

- You don't have a bunch of speeding tickets that hike your insurance rates sky high.

- You don't go through two tanks of gasoline a week cruising the streets.

- Your apartment doesn't catch fire and you lose everything because you didn't have renter's insurance.

- You don't go to movies, concerts, and eat expensive dinners out every night. Everyone needs to have some fun, however, entertainment expenses can bankrupt a budget.

Considering our relatively modest budget, we've already reached $1,750 per month for expenses! Remember, this is money you must **net**. Just because your job pays $1,750 per month doesn't mean you'll be able to meet your expenses. In fact, you would not be able to pay all your bills because federal, state, social security, and local taxes must be paid. These taxes can lessen your take home pay by 15% to 25%, or higher! In other words, if you were earning $1,750 per month, taxes could reduce that amount to less than $1,500 per month. To pay $1,750 in bills per month you'll need to earn approximately $2,065 per month.

| | |
|---|---|
| **Gross Income Needed** | **$2,065** |
| **Less Taxes (15%)** | **($ 310)** |
| **Net Income Needed** | **$1,755** |

Your futuristic budget may need more financial adjustments than your present budget. In the long run, you'll have to decide what expenses you can afford and what expenses you should do away with. The decision is yours.

**Tips for reducing expenses include:**

1. **Lower your rent expense by choosing a less expensive place to live or having a roommate to split rent costs.**

2. **Utilities.** Turn off the televisions, stereos, lights and any

other electronic devices when you're not using them. Turn off or adjust heating and air conditioning thermostat when you leave.

**3.    Reduce the amount of meals you eat away from home.**

**4.    If your transportation costs are high, use public transportation or buy a used car for lower payments and less insurance costs, instead of an expensive new car.** However, when buying a used car, you will need to carefully shop. You don't want to acquire a "lemon" that will cost more to maintain and repair than a newer car that is covered by a warranty. Before making a deal, have a used car inspected by an automobile mechanic recommended by friends or relatives.

**5.    Compare clothing prices at different stores.** You'll want to buy sturdy, well-made clothing for the lowest prices.

**6.    Entertainment expenses can be expensive ... they can make or break your budget.** When you first go out on your own, you'll need every dollar. Many clubs and churches offer discount group rates for entertainment events. Social organizations offer group events that involve inexpensive activities such as biking, hiking, camping, etc. Keep your entertainment costs to a minimum. Be creative in your pursuit of entertainment, and you'll find inexpensive alternatives.

Costs for tuition and books for trade schools, colleges, or universities were not included in our budget. In *Chapter 13 - Higher Education … Your Key To The Future*, we'll discuss financing your education.

Is it difficult to believe that it takes this much money to afford only basic expenses? Supporting yourself is a tremendous financial responsibility.

When you turn eighteen, perhaps breaking out on your own should be postponed for several years in order to obtain a higher education. A higher education that could ensure a well-paying trade or profession would be a wise choice. Get a good education. It will enable you to earn the type of money as an adult that will support the lifestyle to which you want to become accustomed!

**In review:**

- **Track your expenses.**

- **Design a budget that includes income and expenses.**

- **Eliminate unnecessary expenses.**

- **Be creative to increase your income.**

As we've seen, to establish a budget, it's important to know how much you make and spend. An important part of tracking how much you spend is to keep your checking account balanced. In *Chapter 5 - Your Checking Account ... Without The Mystery*, we'll discuss this strategy.

# CHAPTER 5

# YOUR CHECKING ACCOUNT

## Without The Mystery

A convenient way to spend money and establish credit is to have a checking account at a bank, credit union, or savings and loan association. Here are some important checking account tips:

**1.** **There are two parts to a checking account.** The checks you write and the *checkbook register* you keep. The register is a record of every check you write and deposit you make. By keeping your checkbook *reconciled* (known as balanced), you'll know how much money you have in your account.

**2.   Write the amount of the check in your checkbook register.**

**3.   Write the amount of the deposit in your checkbook register.** The idea is to have more $$ deposits in your account than $$ checks written. You'd be surprised how many adults do not understand this concept.

**4.   When you receive your monthly statement from your bank, don't throw the statement away or put it in a drawer never to be found again.** Put the statement in a file folder, specifically for your checking account, and as soon as possible reconcile your checkbook.

To reconcile your checkbook means that total deposits and total checks written on the bank statement match the balance in your checkbook. If you reconcile your bank statement when you receive it, the task will be simple.

There are few things more unpleasant than trying to reconcile a checkbook that has been neglected for three to six months. It's frustrating, time consuming, and simply much easier to reconcile your checkbook every month.

Directions on your bank statement will explain how to reconcile your checkbook with the statement. However, briefly, here's how to reconcile your checking account:

**1.   List and total all checks and other debits in your checkbook register that are not listed on your statement (also include any service charges).**

**2.   List and total all deposits and other credits in your checkbook register that are not listed on your statement (also include interest, if any).**

**3.   To the ending balance listed on your statement, add the total credits listed in #2, and then subtract total debits listed in #1.**

**4.   The dollar amount you reach by adding credits and subtracting debits should be the same amount as your checkbook balance.**

Again, the big secret to keeping your checkbook up to date and accurate, so you know how much you have in your checking account, is to make a habit of reconciling your checking account as soon as possible each month. If you let the months go by, what would normally have taken a few minutes, may take hours!

In addition, most banks offer online banking. Using a computer and mobile devices, you can access your bank account information 24 hours a day, seven days a week.

**Remember to:**

- **Record all checks written in your checkbook register.**

- **Record all deposits in your checkbook register.**

- **Reconcile your checkbook monthly.**

Now that we've discussed how to keep track of your money, let's go on to *Chapter 6 – Taxes and Inflation ... Hidden Costs*, two items that can really take a bite out of your earnings and investments.

# CHAPTER 6

# TAXES & INFLATION

## Hidden Costs

Taxes and inflation are two subjects that many adults do not understand. Your investment strategy must take taxes and inflation into consideration. Why? Because taxes and inflation can take a big bite out of the money you earn and the profit you make on your investments!

Taxes are the monies collected to pay local, state, and federal **expenditures** such as roads, schools, highways, freeways, sewer and water systems. Everyone who earns a salary, owns a business, or makes money on investments pays taxes. Depending upon where you live, the cost of local and state taxes will vary. Also, how much you pay in taxes is determined by your **tax bracket**.

Federal, state, and local taxes take a large bite out of most Americans' paychecks. Simply because you earn $15.00 per hour does not mean your paycheck will equal $15.00 times the number of hours worked. Your paycheck will equal the per hour amount times hours worked, less federal, state, local and *social security taxes*. What remains after taxes are paid is your net income.

## Your gross income minus taxes = net income

Money earned on investments is also taxable since it is considered **unearned income**. You will want a sizeable portion of your investments to earn a return that will pay taxes and still make a reasonable profit for you. There are a few investments that are not entirely taxed or are *tax deferred*. The tax on a traditional *Individual Retirement Account (IRA)* is not paid until the money is withdrawn at retirement. Taxes are also deferred on the interest (income) paid on **annuities** until monies are withdrawn at retirement.

Then there is inflation. Inflation is a factor that should be seriously taken into consideration. **Inflation is the rate of increase, expressed as a percentage, that goods and services increase (or decrease, known as deflation) per year.**

If each year it costs more money to live, it doesn't take long for goods and services to get expensive. Historically, inflation has averaged approximately 3% per year in the United States. For example, at 3% inflation, a yearly college tuition cost of $5,000 would increase over five years to approximately $5,800 per year! That's a total increase of approximately 16% **compounded**.

In recent years, college cost inflation has ranged from 5% to 8% per year. At 6% inflation for five years, that $5,000 yearly tuition increases to approximately $6,700 per year; an increase of approximately 34% compounded!

There is no doubt that inflation can take a financial toll. In *Chapter 13 – Higher Education ... Your Key To The Future*, we will discuss how to overcome the expensive costs of additional schooling.

**In review:**

- **The salary you earn is reduced by federal, state, local and social security taxes.**

- **The income earned from investments is taxed.**

- **When planning future expenses, consider what that product or service may cost in the future due to inflation.**

Now it is time to explore specific types of investments. In *Chapter 7* we will first consider bonds.

# CHAPTER 7

# BONDS

## The Conservative Investment

Many investors consider bonds a safe type of investment. Bonds can be safe and conservative investments. Bonds often are the financial backbone of a city, county, state or even the federal government because they pay for the cost of roads, highways, airports, schools and city renovation. Corporations also issue bonds to finance large *capital* improvements.

In the world of investments, securities are either *debt* or *equity* instruments. A *bond* is a debt instrument and represents a superior promise to repay the bondholder's investment.

A superior promise to pay means a bond investor will be paid her investment before **common stock shareholders** if the company files **bankruptcy**. Therefore, bonds usually are considered a more conservative or safer approach to investing than owning common stock which is an equity investment. However, if a government entity (federal, state, or local government) or corporation is financially in trouble, then its bonds may be poorly rated and considered a high risk. Some bonds are riskier than the common stock of good companies.

**Bonds may be purchased two different ways:**

- A bond may be purchased at a **discount**. A discount is a price below a bond's **face value**, whereby the amount paid the **bondholder** at maturity equals the original $$ invested plus investment return. For example, the face amount of a bond is $1,000. However, because of economic factors, this particular bond sells for $875. If the bond investor pays $875 and waits until maturity to cash the bond, $125 ($1,000 - $875) is the profit received by the investor.

- A bond may also be purchased with a promise to repay the

bondholder's investment plus a specified rate of interest (income). For instance, the bond costs $1,000 and it will pay 5 1/2% interest ($1,000 x 5 1/2%), or $55.

Perhaps you are familiar with United States savings bonds that are backed by the full faith and credit of the United States government. U.S. savings bonds, **U.S. Treasury bills**, **U.S. Treasury notes**, and **U.S. Treasury bonds** are considered a good risk. On the other hand, because of the low risk involved, the rate of return (interest) on U.S. securities can be low compared to other investments.

In *Chapter 12 - Pyramid Basics … The Secret To Investing*, you will learn that usually (but not always) the greater the investment risk, the greater the potential for a higher rate of return. On the other hand, the lower the risk, the more probability for a lower rate of return.

This is not to say that people should not invest in bonds or other low risk investments. On the contrary, it is important for a person's financial portfolio to be well **diversified**.

Savings bonds can be purchased electronically from a web-based system called Treasury Direct. You can also purchase Treasury bills, notes, bonds, floating rate notes (FRNs), and inflation-protected securities (TIPS). For more information go to **www.treasurydirect.gov**.

Before moving on to the next chapter, remember:

- **A bond is a superior promise to repay a bondholder's investment plus interest.**

- **Bonds are generally considered conservative investments.**

- **Bonds help balance the risk of an investment portfolio.**

In *Chapter 8* we will study what powers and runs most corporations in the United States and the world ... stocks!

# CHAPTER 8

# STOCKS

## The Place To Be

In the United States and throughout the world stocks rule!  Tune in to the stock market shows on television to see what I mean.  Today, many people are invested in the stock market.  They are tracking stocks on their mobile devices and computers.  The pace is frantic and hectic.  What effects the companies of the world effects the world we live in, and vice versa.

You may be interested to know that shares of stock represent individual pieces of ownership in a corporation.  When a company needs to raise money, it issues shares of stock for people to purchase through what is known as an ***initial public offering (IPO)***. Initially, the price of stock is determined by the company. Once the stock has been traded (bought and sold) for awhile, ***supply and demand*** takes over, placing a price per share value on the stock.

A company's ***board of directors*** may periodically declare that shareholders be paid a ***dividend*** (income) on each share of stock. I emphasize *may*. Dividends are not required to be paid to shareholders. Some companies rarely pay dividends, preferring to reinvest the profits earned back into the company to promote the company's growth.

**There are two kinds of stock.**

- ***Common stock.*** Owners of common stock have the right to regularly vote for and elect a board of directors to manage the company's business. By electing a board of directors, owners of common stock have a say in the management of a corporation, yet don't have to be involved with the day-to-day activities of operating a business. Common stockholders also vote on corporate policy at annual meetings.

- ***Preferred stock.*** In the last chapter, we discussed how owners of bonds are paid before stock shareholders if the company goes bankrupt. The owners of preferred stock are next in line to be paid in the event of bankruptcy before common stockholders. Preferred stock is issued with a fixed dividend. This is an advantage, as the owners of preferred stock receive dividends before owners of common stock. Preferred stockholders generally do not have voting rights.

Like bonds, company stocks range in their degree of risk. Depending upon the financial stability of a company plus other factors, the stock can range from conservative to high risk.

Investing in stocks of newly formed companies is generally considered riskier than investing in companies that have been around for many years like Amazon, Google, IBM, AT&T, and General Electric.

Companies investing large amounts of capital into new ventures, such as a new telecommunications company or a small pharmaceutical company developing medicines for life-threatening diseases may be considered high risk. While these companies may produce worthwhile products, the large debt they incur may pull down earnings and cash flow for years.

The stock of companies that have a track record of paying their stockholders dividends year after year may be a more conservative investment than the stock of a company that seldom if ever pays dividends.

Sometimes newly formed companies generate large profits for stock market investors. Consider Google, Amazon, Wal-Mart and Microsoft. Initially, each of these companies was starting out in business, new and untested. Years ago, these companies' stock sold for much lower than they do today. By purchasing shares of stock when prices were low and selling when prices rose, investors made large profits.

**Stock market investors make money by purchasing stock when the price is low and selling when the price is high.** Before investing, I recommend that you read many books about the stock market. Several are listed in the *Information Resources* at the back of this book.

The record price and price per share of company stocks, along with other valuable information, can be found online and in the business section of newspapers. To understand stock market quotes, study the explanation for the symbols that accompany the quotes and read books on the subject.

Before investing in a stock, research the company or companies that interest you. How do you make the decision to invest in a company? **Here are suggestions for selecting companies and their stocks. Try this exercise with a friend or classmate.**

**1. Talk to stockbrokers.** Don't be put off ... find someone who will provide you with information and talk to you about stocks and the market.

**2. Select a dozen companies that interest you.** Choose companies whose products you like or use. Pick companies that have been around for many years and some that are relatively new. Research these companies. Locate magazine articles about these companies in the ***Reader's Guide To Periodical Literature***. Read the magazine articles, especially the ones in business magazines. Research the company online. Learn all you can about the company, what it produces, where it conducts business, its history, and how it is managed.

**3.   Choose six of the most interesting companies whose stock you'd like to buy.**

**4.   Limit your investment to an "on paper" investment.** Choose a hypothetical dollar amount to invest and invest an equal dollar amount in each stock.  For example, you plan to hypothetically invest $12,000, you'll be investing $2,000 in each stock ($12,000 /6 stocks).

**5.   On the same day, buy each stock at the price per share listed online.**

**6.   For three to six months track the changes in stock market prices in your notebook.**

**7.   Continue to study your individual stock companies.** Read information about the companies in sources like *Value Line, Standard & Poor's,* and *Morningstar.*  Study company websites.  This will help you understand why the stock price fluctuates with each stock and will give you a much better insight to the world of the stock market.

The above exercise will teach you valuable lessons such as patience.  The ups and downs of the stock market can be volatile.  If the "paper money" had been your hard-earned cash, could you afford to lose a portion or all the money invested? Would you have the patience to ride out the lows and not panic and sell your stock when prices were down?

Stocks can be purchased through full service **stock brokerage** firms and discount brokers. In addition to the stock price, there will be a sales charge to buy and a sales charge when you sell the stock. The sales charge will vary depending upon where you buy and sell the stock. A percentage of the sale price may be charged. However, discount brokerage firms online often charge a flat fee per transaction. Compare fees and services with discount and full-service stock brokerage firms.

When doing business with a full-service stockbroker, you should expect good service to help make stock buying decisions. Fees charged through a full-service stockbroker are usually higher than purchasing stocks from a discount broker. People often get what they pay for.

High brokerage fees will not guarantee that you profit from your stock purchases. Whether you use a full-service stockbroker or invest through a discount broker is a decision that should be based upon your own level of knowledge. This knowledge should include the stock market in general, and the company whose stock you consider buying.

If you have an interest in a company, you should request a copy of its most recent **annual report**. In addition, **research reports** are available from stock brokerage firms and on the Internet for free or for a small fee. Both annual reports and research reports contain valuable information about a company including background information, company developments, and financial strength.

The Dow Jones Industrial Average is the most widely quoted and popular measure of the stock market. The Dow Jones Industrial Average consists of thirty large publicly owned companies based in the United States. These stocks are listed on the **New York Stock Exchange**. Selected as representative of American industry, the thirty stocks are the **blue-chip** shares of large, well-known companies regarded as leaders in their industries and are widely held by individual and **institutional investors**.

If you plan to purchase individual stocks, my advice is to

conduct your own research first. **Questions you need answered include:**

- **What is the company's history?**

- **What are future company plans?**

- **Is the company's stock price unusually high or low?**

- **How long have key company officials been around?** Are any key people expected to leave the company?

- **Has a drastic change in management taken place?**

- **What is the company's dividend paying history?** Has the company paid out too much in dividends, therefore limiting the amount of investment capital available?

- **What are consumer attitudes toward the company and its products?**

- **Do you like the company's products?**

- **Do your friends and family use the company's products?**

- **What is the company's competition?**

No one, I repeat no one, has a crystal ball when it comes to stock market performance. However, since the 1920's the returns generated by stocks have typically exceeded the returns received from fixed interest investments such as bank *certificates of deposit (CD)* and bonds. Many investment gurus say, "the stock market is the place to be!"

**When it comes to stocks remember:**

- **The principle of supply and demand helps establish stock prices.**

- **Buying stock low and selling high is what generates profits for stock market investors.**

- **Do thorough research before investing.**

If you don't have time to research dozens of companies, read the next chapter and consider investing in mutual funds.

# CHAPTER 9

# MUTUAL FUNDS

## Convenient Investing

For the **novice** investor, I recommend mutual funds for the following reasons:

- **Mutual funds are professionally managed by people with years of investment experience.**

- **By their very nature, mutual funds are diversified, a subject that will be covered in depth in *Chapter 12 – Pyramid Basics ... The Secret To Investing*.**

An alternative to owning an individual company's stock is to own shares in a mutual fund.

**A mutual fund is a pool or group of stocks, bonds, or stocks and bonds managed by professional investment managers.** When you own shares of a mutual fund, you own a portion of many companies, fifty to one hundred or more!

**By owning a mutual fund, an investor has the advantage of professional fund management.** Professional management means you don't spend hundreds of hours of your valuable time researching individual companies. Mutual funds are managed by professional investment managers who do the research for you. These professional portfolio managers typically have many years of investment experience. **However, it is your responsibility to research the mutual fund before investing your money in the fund.**

By owning a mutual fund, you are diversified. You are investing in many companies, not placing all your money in only one company's stock. If your money is invested several different ways, the potential for risk is reduced. There are approximately 7,500 mutual funds.

Here are some important factors to consider before investing in one:

1. **How long has the manager managed the fund?**

2. **Is the fund run by one individual or a panel of people?** Each approach has positive and negative aspects.

3. **What is the previous experience of the investment manager?**

4. **The mutual fund has at least a two or three-year history.** While past results are no indication of future results, it is important to have a track record to examine.

5. **How has the mutual fund performed?**

The cost to purchase a mutual fund is generally the fund's *net asset value (**NAV**)* plus the cost of any sales charge. NAV is calculated by subtracting expenses incurred by a mutual fund from the value of a mutual fund's assets, and then dividing that amount by the number of shares in the mutual fund.

Sales charges pay the people who sell mutual funds. Some mutual funds have front end sales charges. These are sales charges that are assessed when the mutual fund is purchased. Other mutual funds have what are referred to as back-end or contingent deferred sales charges.

If you keep your money in the mutual fund for a required number of years, you will not have any sales charges. However, if you do redeem your mutual fund shares before the required number of years have passed, you will be charged the deferred sales charge, which usually declines the more years your money is invested.

An advantage to investing your money in mutual funds over individual company stocks is the professional portfolio management. The mutual fund manager or group of managers track dozens to hundreds of companies. However, they don't work for free. Mutual fund managers are paid from management fees that are assessed against the mutual fund as expenses each year.

In addition, mutual funds charge **annual fees** that cover administrative costs, etc. Different mutual fund companies charge different percentage rates for annual fees and management fees.

Mutual funds are as diverse as the companies they represent. Mutual funds have different investment strategies. Investment strategy determines what types of companies a mutual fund will invest in. Mutual funds may be growth, income, growth and income, international, bonds, foreign, large capital, small capital, socially responsible, or aggressive growth oriented.

**Mutual fund managers invest in the stock of companies that follow their investment strategies.** If a fund has an aggressive growth strategy, monies of the fund may be invested in the stock of companies that are emerging at the time. Emerging companies include high technology companies that reinvest most of their profits back into the company instead of paying the shareholders dividends.

I recommend long-term investing in a mutual fund. At least four to five years are recommended, since most mutual funds have sales charges, whether front end or continent deferred.

Mutual fund share values will fluctuate. Invest for the long-term. Otherwise you might need to sell at a time when the stock market is low and your mutual fund value has declined. Selling at the wrong time could result in a financial loss to you.

Before purchasing any mutual fund, you must be provided a *prospectus* by the mutual fund company or its representative sales person. A mutual fund prospectus includes the investment strategy, types of companies the fund invests in, expenses and fees, and management philosophy.

There are approximately 7,500 mutual funds in existence. Mutual fund companies have several to a hundred or more separate funds that offer the investor any type of investment strategy or philosophy possible. Like stock prices, the share price of a mutual fund can be tracked online.

**Here are tips for mutual fund investments:**

1. **Read the prospectus.**

2. **Ask the mutual fund's sales representative lots of questions.** If the sales representative won't answer your questions, this probably isn't a mutual fund where you want to invest your hard-earned money.

3. **Talk to people you trust.** Ask what mutual funds they recommend. Who are their financial representatives?

4. **Read articles in financial magazines and newspapers about the fund.** You will see a list of some of these publications at the end of this book. Conduct research online.

5. **Watch financial and investment television shows.**

6. **Don't get hooked by the *flavor of the month*.** Research any mutual fund you consider buying.

7. **Make your investment decisions based upon sound research, investigation, and thought.**

8. **Work with a mutual fund representative you like and respect.**

9. **Invest for the long-term.**

**In review:**

- **Mutual funds invest in the stock of dozens to hundreds of companies.**

- **Mutual funds are professionally managed.**

- **Select a mutual fund based upon the fund's investment strategy and your own investment needs.**

Now that we've covered several different investment options, in *Chapter 10* we will explore some ways to protect your *assets*.

# CHAPTER 10

# INSURANCE

## Protect Your Assets

I bet the type of insurance you have heard the most about is car insurance. For the average teen, automobile insurance is expensive, so you may have a negative opinion of insurance.

We've covered automobile insurance in the chapter on budgets. In this chapter, we will discuss life insurance: what it does and how it works.

Life insurance is usually purchased in the event someone dies whose income is necessary for the survival of a family.

**Premiums** are payments made for life insurance. They are paid monthly, quarterly, semi-annually, or annually.

**Whole life insurance** policies are a type of life insurance that accumulates **cash value** as premiums are paid over the years. Whole life insurance premiums typically stay the same year after year. As cash value grows, it can be used by the owner of the insurance policy to help purchase a home, pay for college, or finance retirement. If the cash value is not depleted below the level that pays for the life insurance, the policy stays in force. Therefore, the life insurance protection stays in effect.

**Term life insurance** is a type of life insurance that does not accumulate cash value. Term life insurance premiums for young people are lower than whole life insurance premiums. As the **insured** ages, the cost of premiums may increase, making the cost of term insurance often prohibitively high for people as they get old.

**Here are some tips for selecting an insurance company:**

**1.   Talk to friends, relatives, and people whose opinions you respect.**   Ask them to recommend an insurance agent and insurance company.

**2.   Research the life insurance company.**

**3. Has the company been around a long time?** Fifty years or more indicates that a company is financially strong, has weathered the test of time, and may be around for another fifty years.

**4. Does the life insurance company have a good reputation and a good record of paying *claims*?** How is the company rated? You can learn the answer to this question by researching reports from insurance reporting services such as A.M. Best.

Life insurance can be purchased with investment options that resemble mutual funds. **When purchasing life insurance with investment options:**

- **Read the prospectus.** It's a long read so allow plenty of time to study the prospectus.

- **Study the tract record and returns of the investment options.** How long has it been in existence? How has it performed?

- **Diversify your investment options like you would any other type of investment.** If your other investments are fixed interest or low risk, you may want to balance your portfolio by being moderately or slightly aggressive in your investment approach. Or you may want to invest in several options. For instance, 25% fixed, 25% bonds, 25% stocks, and 25% aggressive investments.

When interest rates are low, stocks often do well. The opposite is also true. In other words, when the stock market is down, interest rates may be high and give you a good return in fixed accounts. Historically the United States has experienced cycles of a booming stock market with low interest rates versus a declining stock market with higher interest rates.

**In review, some important life insurance points include:**

- **Insurance protects the financial assets and earning power of a wage earner.**

- **The cost of purchasing life insurance increases as a person grows older.**

- **For young adults, term life insurance premiums are lower than whole life insurance premiums.**

- **Whole life insurance provides cash values that can be used to pay for college, a home, or retirement.**

- **Life insurance can be purchased with investment options.**

After all this talk about bonds, stocks, mutual funds, and insurance, we'll now explore one of the biggest reasons to save and invest today ... the American dream ... a home!

# CHAPTER 11

# REAL ESTATE

# THE AMERICAN DREAM

Owning your own home (real estate) is the American dream! Consider it this way, everyone needs a place to live ... why not own it?

Most homes can be purchased with approximately 20% down payment (the amount of cash you pay toward the sales price) and financing the remaining balance with a **mortgage**. A mortgage entitles a buyer to make monthly payments for the next ten, twenty or thirty years at a fixed or variable rate of interest, instead of paying all cash for a house, which most people cannot afford.

According to the National Association of Realtors, as of January 2017, the average sales price of existing homes in the United States is $188,900. Therefore, a 20% down payment for the average priced home would equal $37,780, an amount that could take years to save!

Fortunately, government backed programs like those available from the Federal Home Administration (FHA) and the Veterans Administration (VA) enable a home buyer to purchase a home with a smaller down payment than a ***conventional bank mortgage***.

There are also various loan programs, such as first-time home buyer programs, which require as little as 0% to 5% down payment. Talk to a loan officer or mortgage lender at your local bank, savings and loan association, credit union or mortgage company to learn what programs exist in your area.

Some people who want to sell their homes will ***owner-finance***. This means the buyer makes monthly payments to the seller instead of a bank. The seller retains title (ownership) of the house until the loan is paid off.

Sometimes an owner-financed real estate transaction may involve more lenient financing terms. Reasons a home seller would owner-finance are a slow selling real estate market or the property owner wants the income from the loan interest.

When a mortgage loan is paid off, you own the property free and clear.

**When a lender considers an application for a home loan, he will look for the following:**

1.   **The ability of the buyer to repay the loan.**

2.   **Good credit of the buyer.**

3.   **Delinquent or late payment of previous loans.**

4.   **Bankruptcies if any.**

5.   **A proportionate amount of annual income to the sales price of the house.** A rule of thumb is the sales price should be no more than 2 1/2 times your total annual income. For instance, if your income is $24,000 per year, the sales price of your home should be no more than $60,000 ($24,000 x 2.5). With the average home costing $188,900, that's not much of a home in today's real estate market! This rule of thumb explains why many mothers and fathers must both work today to pay for their families' housing needs.

6.   **A proportionate amount of debt to total income.** A

person's monthly debt payments should not exceed 25% of their gross monthly salary. For instance, if your monthly income is $2,000 per month ($24,000 annually) your outstanding monthly debts should not exceed $500 per month ($2,000 x 25%).

**7.    A proportionate amount of monthly debt payments and home mortgage to total income.**    A person's monthly debt payments and house payment combined should not exceed approximately 33% of his or her gross monthly salary. For instance, if your monthly income is $2,000, your monthly debts including house payment should not exceed $660 per month ($2,000 x 33%).

If a person can't meet the above criteria, he may not be able to purchase a home through a banking institution. This person must make a larger down payment or find a less expensive house to purchase. More reason to read *Chapter 13 - Higher Education … Your Key To The Future*, to help you get the highest paying job possible!

If a lender will make a disproportionately high loan compared to your income, you should decline the loan. Remember, it's easier to get into debt than to get out of debt.

I encourage people to keep their house payments as low as

possible and have as much **equity** in the home as possible. A low house payment and more equity can be accomplished by making a larger down payment, purchasing a **fixer-upper**, buying a less expensive house, or doubling up on payments as your income increases.

There is no guarantee what life will bring our way. If it takes two people working in a family to make a house payment and one partner gets laid off from work, it can be difficult to make a home mortgage payment. That's why I recommend as low a house payment as possible *and* paying that mortgage down as soon as possible.

Mortgage payments usually are made for ten, twenty, or thirty years. While a longer pay back term such as thirty years can make for the lowest monthly payment, it can triple the amount of interest, and thus the amount of money you pay for the house in the long run. I generally recommend a payback period of ten to twenty years.

**Tips for buying a house:**

1. **Location, location, location.** That is the secret of home buying. Purchase a home in the best area you can afford.

**2. Find a real estate agent you like and trust.** Real estate agents work on a commission basis. This means they don't get paid until the house sale closes **escrow**. Once you select an agent, respect that person's time and be loyal.

**3. Choose a house with a price tag you can afford.**

**4. Unless you are skilled in the construction trades or have a very close friend or relative who is** ... stay away from fixer-uppers. A fixer-upper could cause more dollars being invested in the house than it's worth.

**5. Buy a house that's compatible with the neighborhood.** This means your house is like other houses in the neighborhood. Do not purchase a home that is over-improved for the neighborhood. An example of over-improvement would be a home with four bedrooms and two bathrooms that is in a neighborhood where the homes are two bedrooms with one bathroom. The value of a superior house tends to be pulled downward by the influence of the smaller, less expensive houses. However, sometimes the value of a smaller, less expensive house will be pulled upward by the influence of larger, more expensive homes in the neighborhood. This could be a good buying opportunity.

**6.   A duplex may also be a good buying opportunity.**  You live in one unit and rent the other side to a ***tenant***.   Thus, your mortgage could partially be paid by your tenant.

Owning your own home is an important step to your financial future.   It may be years before you are ready to take this step. However, owning a home is a very worthwhile long-term goal.

**In review:**

- **A down payment is the amount of money that a home buyer pays toward the purchase price of a home.**

- **A mortgage allows a home buyer to make monthly payments toward the purchase of a home.**

- **Choose a house with a sales price you can afford.**

- **Select a house that's compatible with the neighborhood.**

Now that we have discussed several investment options, read *Chapter 12 – Pyramid Basics … The Secret To Investing,* to learn how to allocate your investment dollars to help reduce investment risk.

# CHAPTER 12

# PYRAMID BASICS

## The Secret To Investing

Many net worth advisors use the pyramid when advising their investment and estate planning clients. I recommend using the pyramid to structure your *investment portfolio*. The pyramid helps create a snapshot of a person's finances.

Draw a large pyramid on a page in your notebook. Start at the bottom of the pyramid and draw a line across the pyramid, approximately one-third way up from the bottom. Next draw a line approximately two-thirds way up from the bottom. Now draw a third line almost at the very top of the pyramid, so that a very small triangle is left. There should now be four sections to your pyramid, resembling the pyramid that "Hal" is holding.

**The bottom portion of the pyramid is considered the base. You should have a solid financial base to build a strong financial future. A good financial base is premised on fixed interest and guaranteed principal investments.**

Fixed interest and guaranteed principal investments include savings accounts, checking accounts, bank certificates of deposit, U.S. savings bonds, and U.S. Treasury bills. In other words, there is a high probability that the money you invest will be returned to you.

Insurance protection, whether it is for a car, home, medical, *disability*, or life insurance, also falls within the base of the pyramid.

Monies invested in the bottom portion of the pyramid are conservative investments. All of us need some conservative investments.

Notice that as you move upward on the pyramid, the shape of the pyramid becomes narrower. The shape of the pyramid illustrates that as the potential for return increases, the potential for loss also increases. Therefore, you may want to limit the amounts you invest in risky areas.

**Now move upward to the next portion of the pyramid. This section is for moderate investments. Moderate investments include bonds, growth and income stocks, and growth and income mutual funds. A home where you reside would also fall within this portion of the pyramid.**

Depending upon the quality of bonds and stocks, they can be conservative, moderate or even aggressive investments. For instance, corporate bonds of a company with a poor record of paying interest on their bonds may be considered an aggressive investment.

**Now move upward to the next portion of the pyramid. This section is for aggressive investments. Aggressive stock investments may not pay dividends to investors. The company may prefer to reinvest profits back into the company so it may grow.**

Aggressive investments are considered riskier than fixed and moderate investments, but have the potential for greater return. Aggressive investments may include the stocks, bonds, or mutual funds of newly formed companies, young companies, and new technology companies.

**Next move into the tiny triangle at the very top of the pyramid. This is known as the area of high risk investments. High risk investments have the potential for large profits. However, the greatest chance of losing some, or all your original investment is in the high-risk area.**

Loss of investment capital is possible with *all* investments, except guaranteed principal investments mentioned in the bottom portion of the pyramid. With high risk investments, the potential for principal loss is *very* high. When investing in the high-risk area, the investor should be very knowledgeable.

High risk investments include **junk bonds** (below investment grade bonds), limited partnerships, rare coins, stamps, **commodities**, and gold and silver bullion. While I do not discourage all high-risk investments, I do urge investor knowledge and relatively small dollar amounts invested in this area. I also recommend sufficient investments in the other levels of the pyramid before venturing into the high-risk category.

There are no cut and dried rules to investing. However, the most tried and true method is diversification, also known as *asset allocation*. Diversification is the process of investing in various sections of the pyramid. If you spread your investment dollars over the different investment categories of the pyramid, the potential for loss is reduced.

In theory, not all investments thrive at once and not all investments decline at the same time. For instance, when growth stocks are up in value, then bonds may be down in value. By allocating your investment dollars into different sections of the pyramid, balance will be achieved and the potential for loss is reduced.

The style of diversification that an investor selects depends upon the individual investor. People who are near retirement risk the loss of needed cash if their investments are too aggressive. If a person is dependent upon the income from investments to maintain her standard of living, a conservative to moderate approach to investing should be considered.

However, being overly conservative today may not be well

advised due to inflation and taxes. If a retired person lives for 20 to 30 more years after retiring and the cost of goods and services continue to inflate (rise) at an annual rate of 3% inflation, after 15 years that individual's cost of living has increased by approximately 56%! If this individual's income does not increase, he or she may face old age with not enough money at a time when life should be free of worries.

Even more reason to start saving and investing at your age! Remember in *Chapter 3 - Saving and Investment ... Time Is On Your Side*, how our $2,000 investment grew to over $145,000? You will be amazed how much your investments can accumulate and grow over years.

For a teenager, with the luxury of time to withstand the ups and downs of the stock market, you can afford moderate or aggressive investments. This is an advantage over someone who chooses to wait until late in life to start investing.

A hybrid form of diversification is a method of investing called **dollar cost averaging**. Instead of investing all your money at the same time, it's more practical to dollar cost average. The practice of dollar cost averaging is a systematic method of contributing a fixed dollar amount or percentage of your income to an investment on a regular basis, say monthly.

For instance, if you decide to invest, $50 per month in ABC Mutual Fund, one month your $50 may buy 2 mutual fund shares when the price per share is $25 per share. However, a month or two later, perhaps the mutual fund is down in price, to say $20 per share; then your $50 will buy 2½ shares. Therefore, you are buying more shares when prices are low and fewer shares when prices are high. By dollar cost averaging, your investment risk is reduced. Dollar cost averaging takes the emotion out of investing and implements a logical plan of investment that's perfect for long-term goals.

**As you make investment decisions remember:**

- **Diversification of your investments may include conservative, moderate, aggressive, and high risk investments.**

- **Diversify your investment portfolio to suit your risk tolerance.**

- **Dollar cost average your investment $$ to help reduce risk.**

Now we will explore one of the best reasons to invest today …

to pay for a career school, college, or university education!

# CHAPTER 13

# HIGHER EDUCATION

## Your Key To The Future

In my opinion, this is the most important chapter in this book. Life for you in the competitive world of the 21st century will require the best education and skills possible. Higher education will be more important than ever to compete for the best jobs that will insure a lifestyle to which you want to become accustomed!

Higher education widens a person's horizons and will be significant in the work place of the 21st century. Specialized and advanced educational degrees will be what it takes to ensure a sound financial future.

Higher education includes trade schools, career schools, community colleges, public and private colleges and universities, medical, dental, and law schools.

Obtaining a higher education is a goal you should pursue whole-heartedly. Mandatory college courses required the first two years will open doors to parts of the world you've never visited. In college, you will establish friendships that will last a lifetime. The friends you eat lunch with in the student union and cram for exams with late into the night, will be contacts and business associates who have connections to the careers and jobs you desire.

**Higher education options include:**

**1. Career and Trade Schools.** Many good professions do not require a four-year degree. The education for non-degreed occupations, which includes white and blue-collar jobs, can be obtained through career schools. These professions require specialized education that is obtained through accredited courses at substantially less expense and time.

**2. Community Colleges.** This is a higher education option that offers opportunities for educational enrichment at affordable prices. These institutions of higher learning often are state and locally supported. By attending local community colleges, students can begin the pursuit of higher education and keep expenses nominal by living at home.

**3. State Colleges and Universities.** These institutions of higher learning offer four years of education at reasonable rates. Master's and doctor's degrees are also offered at these schools.

**4. Private Universities.** These schools generally are not subsidized by taxpayer money, and therefore, cost more to attend. Master's and doctor's degrees may be offered at these schools.

**5. Medical, Dental and Law Schools.** These schools may be part of a university system or an entirely separate school. These schools are expensive.

Without a doubt, the cost of a higher education is a primary consideration when deciding to attend college. In fact, four years or more of additional education can be very expensive.

**Presently tuition and fees for in-state students at two-year public colleges average $3,440 per year; four-year public colleges average $9,410 per year; and four-year private colleges**

**average $32,410 per year.**

In addition to tuition and fee costs, you must consider costs for room and board and books and supplies. **While room and board costs vary throughout the country, the national average total cost of attending a four-year public college is over $28,000 per year. And the average total cost of attending a four-year private college is now over $59,000.**

The costs are higher for students wanting to obtain a master's or doctorate degree, or attend law, dental, or medical school. A student planning to obtain an advanced degree, or attend law or medical school will spend an additional $30,000 and up for each additional year of education.

The cost of four to ten years of higher education amounts to staggering sums. Are you beginning to appreciate the necessity of early planning?

The financing of your advanced education is no different than saving for any other financial investment. Financing a higher education requires setting goals, discipline, and following through with your goals.

**Tips for financing your higher education:**

- **Set aside as much as possible for college on a regular basis.** The sooner the better. Follow the suggestions in *Chapter 4 - Making A Budget* to help you achieve your college savings goals.

- **Suggest relatives contribute to a 529 Plan for you.** A 529 plan is a tax-advantage savings plan designed to encourage saving for future college costs. 529 plans, legally known as "qualified tuition plans," are sponsored by states, state agencies, or educational institutions. They are authorized by Section 529 of the Internal Revenue Code. There are two types of 529 plans: pre-paid tuition plans and college savings plans.

Investing in a 529 plan can provide college savers with special tax benefits. Earnings in 529 plans are not subject to federal tax, and in many cases, state tax, so long as withdrawals are for eligible college expenses such as tuition and room and board. **For more information about 529 plans visit www.sec.gov.**

- **What higher education option do you want to attend?** Career school, community college, public or private college, medical or law school.

- **What schools interest you?** Obtain school information online, from high school guidance counselors, the library, and individual schools. Select six schools.

- **Visit the six schools by your sophomore year of high school.** Contact the school's admissions office to schedule a visit to the campus. During your visit, tour school departments and speak with professors and financial aid officers. Ask lots of questions. These visits will help determine which schools you prefer.

- **During school visits, learn the cost of tuition, room, board, books and supplies per year.** Multiply the annual cost by the number of years you plan to attend school. This will be the approximate cost of attending college before inflation.

- **Attend community college for two years to save money.**

Afterwards, transfer to a state subsidized public university.

- **Instate tuition for resident students is less than attending college as a non-resident.** Attend a school in a state where you are a resident. Residency requirements are important and vary at different schools. Talk to a school counselor if you have any questions as to your residency status.

- **Know deadline dates and application fees for each school you want to attend.**

- **Remember our discussion of inflation in *Chapter 6 – Taxes and Inflation.*** Inflation can also adversely affect the cost of a higher education. If you are several years away from attending college, factor in the cost of inflation.

Inflation rates for college tuition, room and board have varied over the years. Estimates of inflation for college costs have ranged from 2.9% at public colleges and 3.7% at private universities within the last several years. However, the ten-year historical rate of increase has been around 5% per year.

If you do not attend college for four more years, the cost of a higher education could increase by more than 20% (4 years @ 5% inflation) by the time you're ready to attend. Inflation can add tremendously to college costs and must be factored into any college budget. **Use the following College Cost Worksheet and Inflation Factor tables to determine your college costs.**

<u>**College Cost Worksheet**</u>

1. **Number of years until college.**

2. **Current yearly cost of your college.**

3. **Multiply yearly cost by inflation factor (see below).**

4. **Yearly college cost.**

5. **Multiply by number of years you plan to attend.**

6. **Your estimated future college cost.**

## INFLATION FACTORS

| Years Until College | 4% | 6% | 8% |
|---|---|---|---|
| 1 | 1.04 | 1.06 | 1.08 |
| 2 | 1.08 | 1.12 | 1.17 |
| 3 | 1.12 | 1.19 | 1.26 |
| 4 | 1.17 | 1.26 | 1.36 |
| 5 | 1.22 | 1.34 | 1.47 |
| 6 | 1.27 | 1.42 | 1.59 |
| 7 | 1.32 | 1.50 | 1.71 |
| 8 | 1.37 | 1.59 | 1.85 |
| 9 | 1.42 | 1.69 | 2.00 |
| 10 | 1.48 | 1.79 | 2.16 |

It's critical to plan early for the financing of your higher education. However, even the best-laid plans can be derailed by escalating college expenses. Even with early planning, summer jobs, investments, and help from relatives, the money necessary to finance your college education simply may not be available to embark on your freshman year. **This is when the financial aid becomes important.**

Obtaining financial aid is an art form. It requires research, patience, and creativity. **Financial aid may appear elusive. However, there are more grants and scholarships available than you thought possible.**

The remainder of this chapter is devoted to learning how to pay for your higher education with financial aid. Your journey may not be easy. Nevertheless, if you are determined to make a success of your life, there are ways available to get the education you desire.

**Student financial aid includes:**

- **Grants are financial aid that do not require repayment.**

- **Scholarships are not repaid dollar for dollar.** However, this type of financial aid might require an after-graduation commitment of service or employment.

- **Loans.** Many students finance their higher education either partially or completely with student loans. Loans are required to be paid back. Repayment usually does not begin until after graduation.

- **Work Study is financial aid where the student works on or off campus, for minimum wage or higher.**

Since loans must be repaid, obtaining as much financial aid as possible through grants and scholarships is advisable. Competition for financial aid is tough for grants and scholarships. There are limited dollars available for these programs.

Therefore, it is essential to apply to your schools and submit financial aid applications well before deadlines. If you expect to attend college in the fall semester, don't postpone applying for financial aid until a month or two before school begins.

Apply for financial aid nearly a year before you plan to attend college or early in your senior year of high school. Remember deadlines vary at different schools.

To obtain financial aid from federal programs available across the United States, you first must complete the **Free Application for Federal Student Aid (FAFSA).** This application is available at the U.S. Department of Education's FAFSA website: **www.fafsa.ed.gov**.

By completing the FAFSA, you have an opportunity to obtain financial assistance from a variety of sources. Following is a list of Federal Student Financial Aid Programs available with a brief description of each:

**1. Federal Pell Grants.** A Federal Pell Grant does not have to be repaid and is available to students who have not earned bachelors or professional degrees. Pell Grant award amounts are adjusted yearly. The 2016-2017 Pell Grant maximum award was

$5,815 per year.

**Obtaining a Federal Pell Grant and how much you receive depends upon:**

- **Your financial need.**

- **Your cost to attend school.**

- **Your status as a full-time or part-time student.**

- **Your plans to attend school for a full academic year or less.**

2.  **Academic Competitiveness Grants (ACG)** meet the growing need for improved math and science instruction. This grant encourages students to take more challenging courses in high school and to pursue college majors in high demand in the global economy, such as science, mathematics, technology, engineering and critical foreign languages. ACGs provide up to $750 for the first year of undergraduate study and up to $1,300 for the second year of undergraduate study.

3.  **National Science & Mathematics Access to Retain Talent (SMART) Grants** also meet the growing need for improved

math and science instruction. This grant encourages students to take more challenging courses in high school and to pursue college majors in high demand in the global economy, such as science, mathematics, technology, engineering and critical foreign languages. SMART grants provide up to $4,000 for the third, fourth and fifth years of undergraduate study.

**4.    Federal Supplemental Educational Opportunity Grants** (FSEOG) are for undergraduate students with exceptional financial need. Students who receive Pell Grants and have the most financial need will receive FSEOGs first. Grants awarded under this program range between $100 and $4,000 per year depending on your financial need, when you apply, the amount of other aid you get, and the availability of funds at your school.

**5.    Teacher Education Assistance for College and Higher Education (TEACH) Grants** require you to take certain kinds of classes to receive the grant, and then teach within certain requirement fields to keep the grant from turning into a loan. TEACH provides grants up to $4,000 per year.

**6.    Iraq and Afghanistan Service Grants** are eligible to students based upon Pell Grant criteria and death of parent or guardian while serving as a member of the U.S. Armed Forces in Iraq or Afghanistan after the events of 9/11. The maximum award including accompanying Pell Grant award is $5,815.

**7. Federal Work Study (FWS)** provides part-time employment for students with financial need. Students earn the federal minimum wage or higher. Work study jobs are located at school campuses, federal, state or local public agencies, private nonprofit organizations and for-profit organizations.

**8. Federal Perkins Loans** are low interest loans for undergraduate and graduate students. Students attending any one of 1,700 participating institutions, including colleges and career schools, can obtain Perkins Loans. The interest rate for this loan is 5%. The maximum annual loan amount is $5,500 per year for undergraduate students with a total of $27,500. The maximum annual loan amount is $8,000 per year for graduate students with a total of $60,000. Perkins Loans require that repayment begins nine months after you graduate, leave school, or drop below half-time status.

**9. Federal Stafford Loans.** Federally subsidized Stafford

Loans are available to students with financial need remaining after the Expected Family Contribution (EFC), Pell Grants, and financial aid from other sources are subtracted from the annual cost of education.

The federal government pays the interest on the loan while you're in school, for six months after you leave school, and if you qualify to have your payments deferred. Unsubsidized Stafford Loans are available to students who do not have financial need remaining after EFC, Pell Grants, and aid from other sources. The federal government does not pay the interest on an unsubsidized Stafford Loan. Therefore, the student is responsible for all interest payments, which may be paid while attending school or deferred until after graduation.

Stafford Loan amounts presently range from $5,500 to $7,500 per year for *dependent* undergraduate students and $9,500 to $12,500 per year for *independent* undergraduate students. Unsubsidized Stafford Loans are available for graduate students at $20,500 per year. Subsidized and unsubsidized Stafford Loans for undergraduates have a fixed interest rate of 3.76%. Unsubsidized Stafford Loans for graduates have a fixed interest rate of 5.31%.

**10. Federal Direct PLUS Loans** are loans available to parents of dependent undergraduate students enrolled at least half-time at an eligible school and to graduate or professional students enrolled at least half-time at an eligible school in a program leading to a graduate or professional degree or certificate.

Applicants for Plus Loans must not have an adverse credit history and meet the general eligibility requirements for federal student aid. The interest rate is fixed at 6.31% for loans disbursed on or after July 1, 2016 and before July 1, 2017. Repayment of Direct PLUS loans varies.

**Most students are eligible to receive federal financial aid to assist with college or career school costs.** Even though your income, including your parents, is considered, it does not automatically prevent you from receiving federal student aid.

**To be eligible for one or more of the above mentioned federal programs you must:**

- **Qualify to obtain a college or career school education, either by having a high school diploma or General Educational Development (GED) certificate, or by** completing a high school education in a homeschool setting approved under state law.

- Be enrolled or accepted for enrollment as a student in an eligible degree or certificate program.

- Comply with Selective Service registration.

- Have a valid Social Security number.

- Not be in default on a federal student loan and do not owe a refund on a federal grant.

- Use federal student aid only for educational purposes.

- Maintain satisfactory academic progress.

- Be a U.S. citizen or U.S. national, or have a Green Card.

Make your application for federal student aid to **FAFSA** at **www.fafsa.ed.gov**. Create a FSA ID including username and password to get started.

The FAFSA website contains extensive information about the application process and what to expect afterwards. Read this information.

Important information you will need to provide for your FAFSA application includes:

**1.  Your dependent or independent student status.**

**2.  Personal information.**  Your name, legal address, Social Security number (if you don't have a Social Security number, apply for one), parent's Social Security numbers if you are a dependent student, and your driver's license number.

**2.  Federal tax information or tax returns for you and parents if you are a dependent student.**

**3.  Records of untaxed income, such as interest income, child support and veterans noneducation benefits.**

**4.  Asset information for student and parents.**  Assets include cash, savings, and checking accounts.  The market value of real estate and other investments and the amount of debt owed.

Assets also include stocks and bonds, mutual funds, gold and silver bullion.  Your family's personal home is not included.

**5.  List College and Career Schools.**  You must list at least one college or career school to receive your information.  It is advisable to list as many as six.  If you aren't accepted by several schools, you leave room for acceptance from others.

6.  **Sign your FAFSA using your FSA ID.** Upon submission, you will see a confirmation page to know you've successfully submitted your FAFSA. You will also receive email confirmation.

7.  **Make a copy of your FAFSA application for your records.**

If you need assistance filling out the FAFSA, check online for "Help and Hints", consult the FAFSA live technical support staff, and contact the financial aid office at the school you plan to attend.

You can check the status of your FAFSA application online. Within three days to three weeks after you submit your FAFSA, you will receive a summary of the FAFSA data you submitted, known as Student Aid Report (SAR). Review your SAR carefully to make sure the information you submitted on your FAFSA is correct.

The SAR will not state how much financial aid you'll receive. If you applied for admission to a college or career school and have been accepted, and you listed that school on your FAFSA, the school will calculate your aid. Once your schools of choice have received your SAR, the financial aid administrator will determine your financial aid eligibility.

A formula is applied to your FAFSA information to determine your financial need. This formula considers family income, assets, basic living expenses, etc.

The result of the formula will be the Expected Family Contribution (EFC) which indicates how much money you and your family will be expected to contribute toward your education for the forthcoming school year. If your EFC is below a certain level, you will be eligible for federal grants. The EFC will also be used to determine other federal financial aid awards including work study and loans.

**Financial aid is determined by:**

- **Cost of attendance (tuition and fees, room and board, books and supplies, allowances for transportation, etc.)**

- **Expected Family Contribution (EFC).**

- **Federal Pell Grant eligibility.**

- **Aid From Other Sources.**

Your EFC, Pell Grant Eligibility and Aid From Other Sources

are subtracted from the total Cost of Attendance to arrive at the dollar amount of your financial need.

Once determination has been made, the school will send you an electronic or paper aid offer, referred to as an award letter, explaining the type and amount of award you're eligible for at the school.

The timing of the aid offer varies from school to school and could be springtime or as late as immediately before you start school. It depends on when you apply and how the school prefers to schedule awarding of aid. **Therefore, complete your FAFSA as early as possible.**

You may accept or reject the award offered. If you decide not to attend a school, be responsible and contact their financial aid office to inform them of your decision so another deserving student will receive financial aid instead.

In addition to federal financial aid programs, there are other sources of student aid available. These financial aid programs include:

1. **Specialized Field of Study.** If you intend to go into a specialized field, (for example engineering), scholarship monies may

be available through local companies or trade organizations to help curtail the high costs of pursuing certain occupations. However, these types of scholarships may only be available to college juniors and seniors. Check online or contact your school's financial aid office to learn details.

2. **State Scholarships** available through individual states may include teaching scholarships, nursing scholarships and ethnic/minority scholarships. State scholarships are based on scholastic merit, SAT and ACT scores, as well as financial need. This type of scholarship may entail an after-graduation commitment to a stated vocation. To learn about state scholarships available in your state of residence, check online and contact the financial aid office at the schools you consider attending.

3. **National Scholarships** are based on scholastic merit, SAT and ACT scores, as well as financial need. The public library, school financial aid offices, and the web are good sources of information about national scholarships.

4. **ROTC Scholarships.** Air Force, Army, and Naval Reserve Officers Training Corps programs provide scholarship and

professional opportunities for students. These programs may pay for tuition, fees, books, supplies, and provide a monthly tax-free stipend. Participants take ROTC courses as they pursue their university degrees. After graduating and completing ROTC requirements, participants then receive commissions and begin their service in their chosen branch of the armed forces.

**5. Scholarship Searches.** By conducting scholarship searches online, at the college of your choice, or paying a fee to a reputable scholarship search company, you may discover scholarship or loan funds offered by agencies or companies located outside of your city or state. Factors such as your academic goals, your parents' profession, place of residence, or status as a veteran may make you eligible for scholarships or low interest loans.

**College and career school scholarship tips include:**

**1. Type all applications, letters, questionnaires, essays and any other information that is part of the application for scholarship.**

**2. Carefully read all application materials before you submit your application.** Be sure there are no typographical errors, obvious corrections, or messy or crumpled papers if submitted through the mail.

**3. Have a trusted friend, teacher or relative proofread your scholarship application for errors before the application is sent.**

**4. Attend scholarship workshops and talk to people who have received scholarships**. Learn what individual scholarship winners did to receive their awards.

A lot of information is needed to properly fill out financial aid applications. Don't *procrastinate* and expect to complete the application at the last minute. The application will take time, so start early!

Whatever amount of time involved, the financial aid application process is extremely important. After all, financial aid could make the difference between obtaining a higher education or not.

**Remember one vital rule when searching for financial aid:**

- **Consider all sources ... leave no stone unturned!**

Remember, if you don't qualify for a specific type of financial aid your freshman year, you may be eligible in the next year or two.

Once you are over the hurdle of your freshman and sophomore years, there will be more opportunities for financial aid from departmental and specialized field of study sources.

**If you are not able to immediately attend college after high school, don't despair.** Time is on your side! If need be, take a year or two off to save more money. Just don't postpone your decision to attend college too long. Being out of school too long is not in your best interest. You get out of the practice of being a student, and sometimes procrastination leads to permanent neglect. An alternative could be to attend school part-time for a year or two, and still maintain a full-time job.

There should be no excuse for indefinitely postponing a higher education. Search and apply for the grant, scholarship, work study, and loan programs that are available.

Obtaining a higher education may not be easy. No one in this country is guaranteed a higher education. **Therefore, it requires your determination, hard work, and energy to get a higher education.**

There's going to be a lot of competition in the 21st century and those who have the knowledge ... will have the power. If you are willing to work hard and smart, there are ways to get that education. The decision is up to you!

**In summary:**

- **A higher education is the ticket to a successful future.**

- **If you're several years away from college, inflation could increase costs by the time you're ready to attend.**

- **Visit the schools you're interested in attending a year or two before.**

- **There are many sources of financial aid for a higher education; be persistent and creative.**

Now that we've talked about Higher Education, we'll discuss in *Chapter 14* what hopefully happens afterwards ... jobs!

# CHAPTER 14

# JOBS

## Do What You Enjoy

Whether you are looking for a job now or when you graduate from college, there are certain steps to take when job hunting.

**The following are hints and suggestions for finding the job of your dreams!**

- **The best jobs are not always found online or in newspapers.** While these resources are a place to start, consider other alternatives.

- **Contact companies where you'd like to work.** Asking for the name of the person who does the hiring is a good job hunting technique. Follow up by telephoning that person and asking for a job interview.

- **Tell everyone you know that you're looking for a job.** That includes parents, relatives, friends of your parents, teachers, coaches, guidance counselors, ministers, your friends' parents, and people where you shop or do business. In other words, everyone you know should know you're looking for a job. *Networking* is an excellent way to land a good job. This way no source goes unexplored.

- **States and cities have job service centers where you can search for jobs online or in person.** Listings change daily or weekly so check back often. Be persistent. It will take time. The staff at a job service center will learn you are serious and be more likely to remember you and your skills when they receive a job order.

- **Temp agencies can be a gateway to a permanent position.** Register with a temp agency and tackle small part-time jobs. A potential employer has an opportunity to see you work and may offer you a full-time job!

- Search online for jobs. Many websites and search engines specialize in employment opportunities. You can search by job category and location.

- **Social networking.** LinkedIn and Facebook are good sources for establishing a business profile and networking for career opportunities. Use a professional looking photo. List your skills in an easy to read format. Keep your skills current and update as needed. Compare business profiles in the industry you wish to work.

Throughout your job search, be prepared to hear "no" and don't be discouraged. Also, be prepared for "yes." When you do get a "yes" for a job interview, you will need to prepare.

Interviews are very important to getting a job. Your appearance, your behavior, and your ability to communicate are important factors to consider before and during an interview. You only have one chance to make a first impression!

Consider going for a job interview like performing in a theatre play. You must prepare for the interview. By preparing what you say, how you respond to questions, and what questions you ask about the job, you will be more relaxed during the interview.

**Begin your preparation for the interview by writing down the questions you want to ask an employer about the job.** Start with the most important questions first. These will include:

- **What are the job responsibilities?**

- **What does the employer expect from the person hired?**

- **To whom do you report?**

- **What are the hours?**

- **What is the salary?**

- **What are the benefits?** Benefits may include medical insurance, sick leave pay, and vacation time.

It is also very important to summarize to the employer, in as few words as possible, why you want the job and why the company should give you the job.

**In addition, be prepared to answer some questions such as:**

- **Why are you interested in the job?**

- **Why would you be good at the job?**

- **What qualities and skills can you bring to the job?**

Before going to an interview, make a list of the jobs and responsibilities you have held in the past. If you have never held a job before, you can include classes you've attended, after school activities, and references.

**References are a list of people that your prospective employer may contact to learn more about you.** A potential employer may ask a reference about your behavior, your positive and negative characteristics, and your willingness to be responsible and on time.

**Always ask references for permission to use their names.** If you have any question that a person may not vouch for you, don't use that person as a reference. Along with your reference names, include job title, company name, email address, and telephone number. List as many references as possible. At least two or three. As your job and life experiences grow, you'll update and add to your list of references.

Practice really does make perfect. With your list of questions, answers, and statements to the employer, stand in front of a mirror. Look yourself right in the eye, ask your questions and recite your answers into the mirror. Don't be discouraged if you're not comfortable or you forget what to say. Simply practice over and over in front of the mirror.

**Remember to smile.** A smile goes a long way toward putting yourself and the job interviewer at ease.

**Ask a friend or relative to help role play an interview by pretending to be your potential employer.** When role playing, have your friend sit behind a desk or table to make the practice interview realistic.

**Give your "practice employer" a list of questions to ask.** Your job is to respond by answering each question and imagining you are on an actual job interview. Also, ask the "practice employer" questions, so you will feel more comfortable during the actual interview.

It's important to have a neatly typed *resume*. A resume includes your name, address, email address, telephone number, education, work history with dates, hobbies, civic work, social activities, and references.

For a professional looking resume, research resumes online or check out books on resume writing from your library. Some job service agencies and colleges employ people who will help you write a resume for free. For a high paying job, you may want to pay a professional to write your resume.

**The reasons to have a neatly typed resume are:**

**1. A resume looks professional and shows you have a professional attitude about work.**

**2. You have a detailed description of necessary information when you are asked to fill out an application.**

**3. Your resume can be quickly emailed or mailed if you telephone an employer and are told to first submit a resume.**

**Tips for the day of your interview:**

- **Allow yourself plenty of time to reach your interview destination.**

- **Arrive ten minutes early.**

- **Tell the receptionist you are there for an interview.**

- **Take a deep breath to get your nerves under control.**

- **Read over your practice notes and resume.**

- **Relax, smile, and do your best during the interview.**

- **As the interview wraps, smile and thank the employer for the opportunity to interview.**

Don't be discouraged if you don't get the job. Don't give up. Keep going on lots of interviews. And be happy when you do get the job!

If you discover a reference made a favorable impression with an employer, send that person a thank you note. People appreciate being acknowledged for their efforts. They will remember your effort when they receive future calls from potential employers.

When you do get a job, don't go in with the attitude that it's the only job you'll ever have. Upward job mobility is the way of the future. Keep your eyes and ears open. There will be another job opportunity around the corner. Good performance at your present job will be a future job reference!

When considering your employment future, do what you enjoy

and you can't go wrong! Sometimes the best jobs do not pay the most in the beginning. This is often the case in professions such as journalism, publishing, film, and television, to name only a few. A person usually must start at the bottom and work her way up. A job may be exciting and challenging, but it's a difficult choice if you're also faced with a job offer that pays more.

Think long and hard. I don't recommend giving up happiness for a few dollars more and a dead-end job that makes you unhappy. A lower paying job with more chances now for creativity and higher pay in the future may be the route for you to follow.

**In summary:**

- **Tell everyone that you're searching for a job; that's networking!**

- **Design a world class resume.**

- **Role play for your job interview.**

- **Be prepared.**

- **You have one chance to make a first impression.**

- **Find a job that you enjoy!**

If you discover you're not an 8 a.m. to 5 p.m. type of person and you can't find a job you like, perhaps you need to create your own job. **Read on to** *Chapter 15 – You're The Boss.*

# CHAPTER 15

# YOU'RE THE BOSS

## Make It Work For You

More and more people are starting their own businesses. In *Chapter 2 – Setting Goals*, I suggested that shoveling snow on a snow day would be a good way to earn money. If you did this, you would create your own business. **You would be an entrepreneur, a person who organizes and manages a business!**

In the United States, a small business is defined as a business concern that is independently owned and operated, and is not dominate in its field of operation.

The **Small Business Administration (www.sba.gov)** estimates that there are over 28.2 million small businesses in the United States.

Be aware that over 50% of small businesses dissolve within five years of opening. Dissolution includes business sales, mergers, acquisitions, and involuntary closures such as bankruptcies, failures, and terminations.

Don't let that stop you! The lack of proper research, preparation, and working capital is what causes small business owners to fail.

**What type of work do you want to pursue? Where do your talents lie?** Part-time and full-time businesses include graphic design, landscaping, painting houses and fences, website development, walking and grooming pets, office filing and typing, computer repair, babysitting, accounting, house cleaning, research, auto mechanics, law, medicine, accounting, dentistry, or financial planning to name a few. These jobs can be operated by an entrepreneur who is ***self-employed***.

Even if you plan to operate a part-time business, you should treat it as a profession from the beginning. Researching your tax responsibilities or consulting an accountant are first steps to starting your business. You'll need to know your tax responsibilities and advantages.

Self-employed people have tax deductions and tax privileges that aren't available to employed people. For instance, you can deduct costs of operating your business such as office rent, supplies, automobile expenses, tools needed in your business, office furniture, etc. Deducting the costs of operating your business means that the amount of taxes you pay are based on your net income rather than your gross income.

Many businesses can be operated from your home. **Per the Small Business Administration, more than one-half of all U.S. businesses are based out of an owner's home.** Electronic devices, computers, fax machines, and new telecommunications systems make operating a business from home easier than ever.

**The advantages of working from your home include:**

- **Saving money on office rent. Tenant rent can be expensive for a new business on a tight budget.**

- **Saving time and money on transportation.** Not having to commute to and from an office saves money and hundreds of hours per year.

There can be drawbacks such as customers coming to your home and some businesses simply can't be operated from home. **It takes a lot of discipline to work at home.** A business owner can't be distracted, or let the work day be interrupted by poor work habits.

**Ask questions before sinking time or money into your own business.** Read books on the subject, attend seminars, and talk to small business owners in your chosen profession.

**Learn the answers to:**

- **What do I like to do?**

- **Would people pay me for this service?**

- **What do business owners like and dislike about their profession?** I once thought I'd like to be an attorney. After working for several and talking to attorneys, I decided it was not a profession I wanted to pursue.

- **What education is required?** Some self-employed professions require college degrees, extensive education, or special licenses or designations.

- **How did business owners get started?**

- **Ask business owners for suggestions and recommendations for being self-employed.**

- **What mistakes have business owners made in their businesses?**

- **What does it cost to get started?**

- **How do business owners advertise and market their businesses?**

- **What would business owners do differently?**

The Small Business Administration and local community colleges are good sources of information about owning and operating your own business.

If starting your own business is intriguing, read lots of books on the subject and magazines for the self-employed. Sources are listed in the *Information Resources* at the back of this book.

By doing research, talking to business professionals, and reading books and magazine articles on your chosen profession, you'll decide whether you have what it takes to be a business owner.

In summary:

- Business owners don't plan to fail, they may fail to plan.

- Obtain help for your business from organizations like community colleges and the Small Business Administration.

- Treat your business as a profession from the start.

- Do what you love, and you'll love what you do!

Whether you are a business owner or have a salary paying job, one item that you will need at one time or another in your life is credit. Read on to the next chapter and learn how to get and keep good credit.

# CHAPTER 16

# CREDIT & CREDIT CARDS

## A Word of Caution

Good credit is a very good thing. By opening a checking account or savings account, you have established a form of credit.

To establish further credit, you can approach the banker where you have your checking or savings account and apply for a small loan ... say $100 to $500. The bank will require a completed application and some proof of your ability to repay the loan. You may also be able to get a loan if a relative co-signs the loan (promises to pay if you don't).

You will establish good credit by making payments on time

every month. A good payment history increases your chances of getting a larger loan in the future.

For many teenagers, as well as adults, your first major loan is for an automobile. You can finance a car through your bank, lending institution, or even the car dealership.

Many department and retail stores will extend credit to customers purchasing their products. However, interest rates on these consumer accounts can be very high and should be paid off entirely each month.

Seriously explore the world of borrowing money. You should know that negative consequences can result from being slow with payments or failing to repay the loan. Unfortunately, once a person gets into debt, getting out of debt can be difficult.

In the United States, 819,159 bankruptcies were filed in the year ending June 30, 2016. Compare that figure to 1.6 million bankruptcies filed in the year ending June 30, 2005. While this is a significant improvement, today, many Americans are seriously in debt. If handled improperly, credit cards can lead to serious financial problems.

Having good credit, and I emphasis *good* credit, is a very positive situation. **With good credit, a person can buy a car or a house with equal monthly payments.** This is a privilege because most people cannot afford to pay all cash for a car, much less a house. The misuse of credit can lead to financial disaster.

In *Chapter 6* we discussed how inflation compounding year after year can significantly increase your college costs. A similar situation develops with inappropriate borrowing. If people overspend with credit cards and do not pay off balances each month, they can find themselves in the position of paying out more than they earn. Many adults do not understand that by making only minimum payments on credit cards, it takes years to pay off the balance owed.

**Credit card guidelines include:**

**1. Avoid applying for multiple credit cards.** The lending institution where you bank can be a good source for one credit card.

**2. Compare credit card company interest rates and rewards**. Credit card companies are competitive. They want your business. Many credit card companies charge interest rates ranging from 15% to 21% per year! By comparing, you will find a credit card company with lower interest rates and a better rewards program.

**3. Charge only what you can pay off within one to three months.** It's much better to pay off your credit card balance every month. Paying only the minimum monthly payment (approximately 2% of the balance) as many adults do, can lead to serious problems.

**4. Be cautious if you receive unsolicited credit card offers in the mail.** High interest rates and annual fees may be attached to this card.

Credit card companies are in the business of making money. They may not diligently screen applications and will extend more credit than a person can handle.

**Remember our saying, "people don't plan to fail, they fail to plan."** Treat borrowing money and credit cards like any investment venture. If your investments are paying 10% and your credit cards cost you 20% interest, what's wrong with this picture?

Here's a tip that you can share with your parents. If they have high interest on credit cards, suggest they call their credit card companies and negotiate lower interest rates. They can tell the credit card company that they are prepared to take their business (and the credit card company's way of making a living) to another credit card company with more competitive (lower) interest rates. Some credit card companies will lower interest rates and waive annual fees on the spot! Suggest your parents give it a try. It's worth a telephone call.

Be as cautious with your borrowing habits as you are with your savings and investments. Credit card debt has reached epidemic proportions in this country. Many people owe $30,000, $50,000, or more in credit card debt. Don't let yourself become part of that statistic! With high rates of interest, it could take 10 years or more to pay off credit cards if only the minimum monthly payment is made.

**Avoid the credit card merry-go-round:**

- **Pay off credit card balances within one to three months.**

- **Take an additional job, say part-time, to pay off credit cards as soon as possible.**

- **Negotiate the interest rates on credit cards.** For instance, if you have a credit card balance of $5,000 at 18% interest, you would pay approximately $900 a year in interest! If you can negotiate a new interest rate for 11%, the amount of interest paid would be lowered to $550 per year. That's a huge savings.

Lower interest rates on credit card debt can save a person hundreds to thousands of dollars every year. I suggest that any money saved by lower interest rates be used to pay the balance down on credit cards. That extra payment can help reduce the time it takes to pay off credit card debt.

**In review, when dealing with credit and credit cards:**

- **Establish good credit with a small loan and you will increase your ability to obtain larger loans to purchase a car, house, or business.**

- **Build good credit by making payments on time.**

- **Charge only what you can pay off within one to three months.**

Enough on words of caution ... let's now consider your financial *philosophy*. Read on.

# CHAPTER 17

# WRAPPING IT UP

## The Can-Do Philosophy

Here we are at the end of our money management adventure. Do you know more about money and finances now? Do you think you know *all* there is to know about money management and investments? Well, you don't! As mentioned at the start, this book is only a beginning when it comes to money management and the accumulation of wealth. What you have learned to this point are the basics. The basics can be very helpful, although it's up to you to proceed further with your money management education. You will find a lot of sources of information available to you.

There are publications which can give you useful and fun information about investing. There are websites and magazines devoted to tips on saving, investing, and making money. The shelves of bookstores and libraries are full of books on how to invest in stocks, bonds, mutual funds, real estate ventures, getting into college, getting a job, budgeting and financing your first car, a college education, or a home.

Your local library is virtually a gold mine of information … free of charge! You will find printed and online financial newspapers and magazines very helpful.

I encourage you to read the *Information Resources* section at the end of this book. Check out as many books as possible from your library and read them. If you get only one idea from each book, you will be very, very rich in investment knowledge. Invest your time learning about finances and you will positively invest in your future!

There are also television programs devoted to the exploration of investments. A favorite of mine is Jim Cramer's *Mad Money* television show. Bloomberg and CNBC televise shows devoted to the subject of investments. Throughout the business day you will see stock market quotes across the bottom of the television screen and news-style programs with guest experts answering investment questions.

Read biographies of the popular mutual fund managers such as Warren Buffett and Peter Lynch. It's enlightening to learn how they got to where they are today managing mutual funds worth billions of dollars!

City newspapers have business sections which contain stock market and mutual fund quotes and investment advice.

Get acquainted with a stockbroker, a mutual fund specialist, or financial planner. If you have a class project or paper to write, many business people will be happy to spend time answering your questions.

At first, in your quest for more knowledge about investments, the material you read or the television programs you watch may seem confusing. If you are patient and continue to read financial magazines and books, and watch financial televisions programs, eventually the investment lingo will make sense. That's when money management, finances and investing become fun!

My wish is that you will continue your search for information about investments and the management of money. By being persistent and inquisitive you shall reap the financial benefits. Best wishes and success!

# GLOSSARY

A dictionary is a wonderful source of information. I recommend that you use one daily to learn the meaning of words. This glossary has been included to help you understand the advice and principles taught in this book.

**annual fees** – the yearly fees paid by the owner of a mutual fund to the mutual fund to cover expenses such as administration costs. Also, yearly fees charged by credit card companies.

**annual report** – a statement published yearly regarding a company's state of affairs.

**annuities** – investments yielding fixed payments during the annuity owner's life, for a certain number of years, or indefinitely.

**asset allocation** – the process of dividing your investment dollars among several different investment options to help reduce investment risk.

**assets** - the value of possessions owned by a person, including cash, savings, stocks, bonds, gold and silver bullion, real estate and other investments.

**balanced** – the state of things being equal.

**bankruptcy** – the state of being legally declared unable to pay your debts, whereby your property is administered for the benefit of creditors and divided among them.

**blue chip** – terminology used to explain large, well-known companies considered to be leaders in their industry.

**board of directors** – a group of individuals chosen to direct the affairs of a corporation or institution.

**bondholder** – a person who owns a bond issued by a company, government, or person.

**bonds** – interest bearing certificates issued by companies or governments promising to pay a specific sum on a specific date.

**bullion** – gold or silver cast into a bar or other convenient shape.

**cash value** – the amount of money that is available to an insured for his own use, while keeping the insurance coverage in effect.

**capital** – most important; having to do with wealth; property and money owned by a person or company.

**certificate of deposit (CD**) – a bank certificate acknowledging the receipt of a specified sum of money in a special kind of time deposit drawing interest and requiring written notice for withdrawal.

**checkbook register** – the written record of checks written and deposits made in a checking account.

**claims** – demands for insurance coverage by insureds when losses occur.

**commodities** – basic items or staple products traded, such as agricultural products.

**common stock** – an investment that represents ownership in a corporation. There is no definite dividend rate and it does not have the privileges of preferred stock, but usually gives an owner a vote at shareholders' meetings in proportion to shares owned.

**common stock shareholders** – the owners of common shares of a company's stock.

**compounded** – interest on the original interest amount plus the accumulated interest which accrues at regular intervals.

**conventional bank mortgage** – a mortgage obtained through a recognized banking institution with interest rates that are the going rate.

**credit** – money made available by a bank or other lending institution.

**debits** – entries or checks written in a checkbook register that decrease the amount of money in said checking account.

**debt instrument** - an investment that is an evidence of debt issued by corporations and governments.

**dependent** - a student who relies upon parents or guardians for financial support.

**disability** – that which disables, as an illness or injury.

**discount** - the price at which a bond sells that is below its face amount.

**disposable income** – income that is available to spend after all taxes have been paid.

**diversified** – to vary or divide up investments among different companies, securities, types of investments, etc. A diversified investment portfolio can help reduce investment risk.

**dividend** – money paid to stockholders as income for investing in a company.

**dollar cost averaging** – the practice of contributing a specified dollar amount to an investment on a regular basis, say monthly. In principle, the cost of buying an investment averages, so a person is not always buying at a high or low price per share.

**Dow Jones Industrial Average** – 30 highly capitalized companies, primarily from heavy industry, listed on the New York Stock Exchange.

**down payment** – the amount of cash a buyer pays toward the total sales price of a home. Usually the dollar amount remaining (sales price minus down payment) will be covered by a home mortgage.

**duplex house** – a house consisting of two separate family units.

**ending balance** – the amount of money in your checking account as of the date of the bank's monthly statement.

**entrepreneur** – a person who organizes and manages a business undertaking, assuming the risk for the sake of the profit.

**equity** – the value of a property beyond the total amount owed on it in mortgages, liens, etc.

**equity instrument** - an investment that is evidenced by ownership in a corporation.

**escrow** – a written agreement, as a bond or deed, put in the care of a third party and not delivered or put in effect until certain conditions are fulfilled.

**expenditures** – expenses.

**face amount** - the amount of a bond on which interest is calculated.

**fixer-upper** – a house that needs improvements made, such as repairs and remodeling, to reach its full potential.

**flavor of the month** – a mutual fund that is favored by investors due to a large amount of publicity.

**frivolous** – of little value or importance; trifling; trivial.

**gross income** – total income earned before taxes are taken out.

**hypothetical** – based on, involving, or having the nature of, a hypothesis; assumed; supposed.

**implementing** – to carry into effect; fulfill; accomplish.

**independent** – a college student who is not reliant upon parents or guardians for his/her source of income.

**inflation** - an increase in the price of goods and services expressed as a percentage rate.

**initial public offering (IPO)** - shares of stock issued for people to purchase when a company needs to raise money.

**institutional investors** – investors such as large banks and insurance companies who invest very large sums of money and often are given preferential treatment regarding sales charges, etc.

**insured** – a person whose life, property, etc., is insured against loss.

**investment portfolio** – the investments of an individual or entity.

**junk bonds** – types of bonds generally considered to be inferior; below investment grade.

**maturity** – the time at which a bond, etc., becomes due.

**mortgage** – the pledging of property to a creditor as security for the payment of a debt.

**mutual funds** – a pooling of investors' money that is invested in various securities as determined by a trust or corporation's objectives.

**negotiate** – decide, settle, or conclude (a personal or business transaction).

**net** – the amount of money remaining after taxes are paid.

**net asset value (NAV)** – the value of a mutual fund's shares calculated by subtracting expenses incurred by a mutual fund from the value of a mutual fund's assets, and then dividing that amount by the number of shares in the mutual fund.

**net gain** – income or profit remaining after expenses have been deducted.

**net income** – the amount of income remaining after all taxes are paid.

**net loss** – the amount of loss after all expenses are subtracted.

**networking** - exchanging ideas and information with a group of people or individuals.

**net worth advisor** - a person who advises investors on financial matters.

**New York Stock Exchange** - the organization that regulates matters related to trading New York Stock Exchange listed securities and the conduct of its members.

**novice** – a person who is a beginner to an activity or occupation.

**owner-finance** – a real estate loan where the property owner accepts payments (and retains ownership of the property) from the buyer until the property is completely paid.

**philosophy** – theory or logical analysis of the principles underlying conduct, thought, knowledge, and the nature of the universe; included in philosophy are ethics, logic, metaphysics, etc.

**preferred stock** – stock on which dividends must be paid before those of common stock; it usually also receives preference in the distribution of assets.

**premiums** – systematic payments made to cover the cost of insurance. Premiums may be paid monthly, quarterly, semi-annually, or annually.

**principal** – the amount of a debt, investment, etc., minus the interest, or on which interest is computed; the face value of a stock or bond.

**procrastinate** – to put off doing something unpleasant or burdensome until a future time; to postpone.

**prospectus** – a written statement outlining the main features of a mutual fund. A prospectus may include investment strategy, expenses, fees, and management philosophy.

***Reader's Guide To Periodical Literature*** – a reference tool, available through libraries, to recently published articles in periodical magazines and scholarly journals, organized by article subject.

**reconcile** - determine the amount in your checking account by adding and subtracting deposits and checks written as compared with the monthly written statement received from your bank.

**research report** – a report of valuable information about the operation, credit worthiness, and management of a company.

**resume** – a summary of a job applicant's personal information, education, employment experience, and references.

**return** – the amount of interest or income received on an investment.

**Individual Retirement Account (IRA)** – a type of retirement investment where the amount invested and accumulated interest are tax deferred.

**self-employed** – a person who owns her own business.

**shareholders** – owners of a company's stock.

**Small Business Administration** – an organization that assists owners of small businesses with the operation of their businesses.

**socially responsible** - a type of mutual fund that invests only in companies that are considered friendly to the environment and society in general. Socially responsible funds often do not include tobacco or liquor companies.

**social security taxes** – taxes that are withheld from a person's income that help pay for disability and retirement benefits.

**stock** - an individual ownership in a company evidenced by a certificate.

**stock brokerage** – a company that acts as an agent in the buying and selling of stocks and bonds.

**subsidies** – a grant of money, often from government sources, to a private enterprise considered of benefit to the public.

**supply and demand** – an economic theory that the quantity of goods or services (supply) offered for sale at a given price is fueled by the desire to own or use (demand) that product or service.

**tax bracket** – the percentage of taxes a person pays based upon annual income less allowable deductions.

**tax deferred** – a type of investment where taxes are not paid until the investment is cashed in.

**tenant** – a person who pays rent to occupy or use a building or land.

**term life insurance** - a type of life insurance that does not accumulate cash value. Because term life insurance premiums only pay for the cost of insurance, premiums are usually low when a person is a young age and increase as a person ages.

**U.S. Treasury bills** (also known as T-bills) – a short-term obligation of the U.S. Treasury, sold in terms ranging from a few days to 26 weeks, bearing no interest and sold periodically on the open market on a discount basis.

**U.S. Treasury notes** - a medium-term fixed interest U.S. government debt security having maturities of one to ten years.

**U.S. Treasury bonds** - a long-term fixed interest U.S. government debt security having maturities of ten to thirty years.

**unearned income** – income that a person earns from sources such as stocks, bonds, mutual funds, and savings accounts.

**whole life insurance** – a type of life insurance that accumulates cash value that can be used by the insured. Whole life insurance premiums generally stay the same as the insured ages.

**yin and yang** – in Chinese philosophy, yin is the passive, negative, feminine force or principle in the universe contrasted with and complementary to yang, the active, positive, masculine force or principle in the universe. Chinese philosophy states that for the universe (and your life) to function properly, a balancing of yin and yang must be in effect.

# INFORMATION RESOURCES

There are thousands of personal finance, investment, money management and real estate books, newspapers and magazines; websites; and television shows. Read as many as you can.

## Books

Buffet, Warren. *How To Start Your Very First Business.* Downtown Bookworks, 2015.

Canfield, Jack. *The Success Principles.* HarperCollins Publishers, 2016.

Cramer, James. *Get Rich Carefully.* Penguin Publishing Group, 2014.

Hagstrom, Robert G. *The Warren Buffett Way.* Wiley, 2013.

Hanson, Charles W. *Resume Writing 2017.* CreateSpace Publishing, 2016.

Hill, Napolean. *Think and Grow Rich!* The Napolean Hill Think and Grow Rich Society, 2012.

Lynch, Peter. *One Up On Wall Street.* Simon & Schuster, 2000.

Mettling, Stephen and Cusic, David. *Principles of Real Estate Practice.* CreateSpace Publishing, 2014.

Osteen, Joel. *Think Better, Live Better.* Faithwords, 2016.

Robbins, Tony. *Unshakeable: Your Financial Freedom Playbook.* Simon & Schuster, 2017.

Yate, Martin. *Knock'em Dead 2017: The Ultimate Job Search Guide.* Adams Media, 2016.

## **Magazines & Newspapers (print & web based)**

*Barron's*
*Bloomberg Business Week*
*Business Week*
*Consumer Reports*
*The Economist*
*Entrepreneur*
*Financial Times*
*Forbes*
*Fortune*
*Inc.*
*Investment Advisor*
*Investment Week*
*Investor's Business Daily*
*Kiplinger's Personal Finance*
*Money*
*Money Observer*
*Newsweek*
*Time*
*SmartMoney*
*U.S. News & World Report*
*The Wall Street Journal*

## **Television**

*Bloomberg News*
*CNBC*
*Jim Cramer's Mad Money*

www.ingramcontent.com/pod-product-compliance
Lightning Source LLC
Chambersburg PA
CBHW070731220326
41598CB00024BA/3384